THE LEBANON
DIARIES

The Lebanon Diaries

An Irish Soldier's Story

by Martin Malone

maverick
house

Published by Maverick House, Main Street, Dunshaughlin, Co. Meath, Ireland.
Maverick House SE Asia, 440 Sukhumvit Road, Washington Square, Klongton, Klongtoey, Bangkok 10110, Thailand.

www.maverickhouse.com
email: info@maverickhouse.com

ISBN 1-905379-25-0
978-1-905379-25-5

£150,991

Printed and bound by ColourBooks Ltd.
5 4 3 2 1

The paper used in this book comes from wood pulp of managed forests. For every tree felled at least one tree is planted, thereby renewing natural resources.

A CIP catalogue record for this book is available from the British Library.

DEDICATION

This book is dedicated to those who are still paying for the sacrifice, still quietly bleeding tears...

And so we hide our dead in silent shade,
And hasten back to life, and life's parade;
Plunge into duty; grind in labour's mill.
Till the eye sees not, and the heart is still...

From 'After the Soldier's Funeral'
by Samuel Francis Smith:1800-95

ACKNOWLEDGEMENTS

Thank you to the very many soldiers of all nationalities with whom I served abroad, for their friendship, and for making my tours of duty so pleasant and memorable. It has been my pleasure to serve with you. In particular, my thanks go to the Irish Military Police of all ranks. Each tour was like being away with family, so strong was the support and camaraderie.

Author's Note

Little did I think as I began to write this book some months ago that the world's attention would yet again be focused on the Israeli-Lebanon border. August 2006, and the war shows no sign of slackening its grim intensity.

As usual in war it is the innocent civilian who suffers the most. To date a total of 900 civilians have been killed in the conflict, a third of whom were children. The image, amateur video footage, of a child of five or six dressed in shorts and lime-green T-shirt, stiff in the arms of his father as he was put to rest in a mass grave, was soul-sickening.

These images are familiar to me, UN soldiers, and the world at large. For some few years it appeared as though peace had at last come to that region—we know now that the Hezbollah used the peaceful period to consolidate and strengthen their military capacity. The incident that sparked this latest violence was the abduction of two Israeli soldiers, but this happened to other Israeli soldiers in October 2000 and yet no war developed.

I know people on both sides of the border. I remain impartial, understanding if not agreeing with the Israeli response to acts of terrorism. The Hezbollah organisation understands the Israeli mindset, i.e. The Israeli will shoot ten of his own people dead in order to kill a lone terrorist. The Hezbollah loosen their rockets from positions close to civilian and UN locations, drawing Israeli artillery into raining shells upon them, the effect often catastrophic.

The TV news brings to my notice more deaths in South Lebanon and in Israel. The damage to the infrastructure of Lebanon has set the country back decades—diplomatic moves to end the violence appear sluggish and without enthusiasm for any immediate end. I think of the people on both sides of the border—there are no winners in this war. And peace I believe, to borrow from Yeats, will arrive '… dropping slow.' A minute of war is a war already too long …

PROLOGUE

In a divided land where people are intent on destroying each other, all the UN does is bear testament, witness, to what's going on and give as much humanitarian aid as possible to those in trouble. But we're not fulfilling our mandate: to help the Lebanese Government re-establish its authority in the south, to oversee the Israeli withdrawal to the internationally recognised frontier. Well, the Hezbollah are part of the Lebanese Government and are intent on wrestling control of the region from the Israelis. They don't need our help.

The UN are pig in the middle and can't do a thing to prevent innocent people being used as pawns by both sides in the war. As a force they aren't strong enough to do what should be done—to prevent the fighting. They shouldn't be here, I think. It's time to move on. They're not fuckin' wanted; instead of finding a solution to the problem they have become part of the problem.

This is only my opinion. My views don't reflect official UN or Army policy. In fact, many in the Defence Forces and the United Nations would disagree with me but I believe it is time for the UN to withdraw from Lebanon, or find another way to bring about peace.

I see Lebanon in its present throes, as a war ground. As the song says, its skies are burning. Children are being lowered into graves, and in me there's a pain and like the worst of pains it's deep, and cuts at the bone and heart. For I know the land, the people. I know them so well. I know the faces behind the statistics. Part of me is in Lebanon, part of Lebanon is in me. I soldiered there … and I want to tell you about how I came to do that, to serve in Lebanon, and the ramifications that such service had on my personal life, its lasting effects.

* * *

The tricolour flag on top of the Water Tower, the Curragh Camp's dominant feature, edged down its mast to a half-way point and stayed put. The soldier whose hands were on the cord, guiding the flag into position, was hidden from view by tall parapets. It was a sad decline as its lowering signalled a fact: the death of a soldier or a dignitary, a civic guard.

Rifle reports echoed from the ranges, carried on the sharp May breeze.

'The flag's at half-mast…?' I said, wondering aloud.

'What?' 09 said, squinting upwards.

'Oh, the Leb,' 09 said. 'Someone was killed there, Bra-Shit. From the west he was—I heard his name but I forget it. God bless the family. The news is probably eating them now, as we speak.'

We lapsed into a respectful silence.

It was 1982. The country held in the grip of depression, for many the army proved to be an economic bolt-hole. However, in the cash-strapped Ireland of then, even the army was instructed to close its doors by a Government intent on reining in public expenditure. Thus, orders were given to curtail promotions and recruitment with the exception of the officer corp and trade apprenticeships – decisions that would later have a profoundly stagnating effect on the force. An unnatural hiatus was created from which the army is still recovering. For years there was no intake of recruits, no new blood … new faces belonging to those of young officers and apprentices—a ridiculous situation that allowed develop a high age profile in the other ranks and a glut of commissioned officers for whom there was little or no prospect of promotion.

Low morale, low pay, caught in a rank system which was a ladder that had no rungs, bar the one your foot stood on.

09 drew on his cigarette, flicked the ash to the ground. He wore green fatigues and his black beret had a sharply defined crease, rising in an apex above the cap badge, mildly alluding to a grotto effect. He was thinking of a family in distress.

We both were.

'Have you been to the Leb?' I said.

He shook his head, 'No. The Congo and Cyprus…'

Then he looked at me and said, 'But you'll go.'

'I won't.'

'Ah, you will, you will…'

How right he was … five times right.

CHAPTER 1

I come from a soldiering background. A French great-grandmother lost a brother who was serving in the French army during World War I. A great-grandfather served in India and brought home a crib and associated figurines which are extant and displayed each Christmas in my parent's home. An uncle served eight years in the British army. My grandfathers contributed 60 years of service between them in the Irish Defence Forces. Neither had the opportunity to serve their country abroad. I've a brother who served for 21 years in the PDF, the Permanent Defence Force (professional and full-time army), and a nephew who is currently serving. So, soldiering is in the blood. Mostly every second generation.

I was a year married before I joined the army. My wife Bernadette grew up in the Curragh Camp and was aware of the demands that a military life brought to a relationship. She had a good family network about her that proved vital and necessary when I eventually made up my mind to begin volunteering and commenced to serve in Lebanon and elsewhere.

The process of the decision was a long and lengthy one. I had abhorred the notion of leaving home—six months looked such an inordinately long time to be away. Is it natural for a married man to haul his roots and leave his family for half a year? Natural or not I was to discover that it was a necessary practice for many couples, if they wanted an improved lifestyle.

Working a three-shift system on the factory floor, I was caught up in a daily grinding lifestyle and the army I soon discovered wasn't the type of job where you could take your work schedule for granted. A civvie can refuse to work overtime whereas in the army the word overtime didn't exist. Army life was neither too difficult nor too easy, the long hours required to spend on duty were boring and tedious. MP mobile patrols were better than being cooped up in an installation such as a guard room or an ammunition depot. You were out and about, out from under the eye—and this was something I appreciated about being a Military Policeman, in comparison to say, an infantryman: you were afforded scope and freedom, permitted to use a large degree of initiative. At home the MP was treated with less respect than his job merited, though the authorities and most of the officers frowned upon this. In Lebanon and elsewhere I was to discover that the MP had a decent and appropriate measure of respect afforded to him.

So often I would listen to the lads who had just returned from overseas discuss their trips. Friends in the unit came and went and you mightn't get to see each other for a year. Most returned home with tans as positive as their experience had been, while a few spoke of having endured, 'A bad trip.'

A tour of duty was bad if someone in the battalion had been killed or seriously injured. An air of depression would hang like a pall over the whole battalion; the circumstances of the incident discussed at length and then held in silence, each soldier keeping his thoughts to himself. Bad if an officer or a senior NCO acted like an arsehole, in the sense that he made life unnecessarily difficult for his platoon or section. He could for instance have his platoon picking up papers in the midday sun, or painting stones white, or hold parades for uniform inspection and kit or locker inspections at inconvenient times. Silly things done to instil discipline or to keep the soldier busy, for the sake of it—flimsy reasons.

***

At that time there was a three to four-year waiting period for an opportunity to serve abroad. What one did was calculate the number applying, the position of seniority you held within the unit and factor in the result. Some fellas had dirty bibs and though they kept putting their names forward it was a given that they would never wear the blue beret.

The reason so many volunteered for Lebanon is easy to fathom and comprises many intermingling strands: money, adventure, sunshine, break from barrack life—to be shut of patrolling the Camp by foot or Land Rover on cold winter nights, manoeuvres in the Glen of Imaal, parades and spit-shined boots, the painting of white webbing, the cleaning of brass, fastened to a barrier on a frosty night for hours, a separation of convenience in a troubled marriage, an attempted repair through absence.

As I write I recall one of the guys in the duty room playing a cassette tape of rocket fire and shell rounds exploding close to his position and a lad standing beside the turf fire shaking his head and saying, 'I'd never go there, no fuckin' way—are ye mad … mad bastards those Arabs—like fuckin' dogs biting at the wind.'

There was the question of danger, but the old sweats would say, 'If you're meant to drown you won't be shot,' and this made sense and had a calming affect on younger fellas who'd have been anxious about the stories they'd heard—some the public got to hear of and others they didn't. The hidden details, the inmost aspects of violent death ...

Bi-annually an empty list appeared on the unit notice board, requesting applications to be submitted hereunder for UNIFIL, the acronym for United Nations Interim Force in Lebanon—as it turned out, an interim of 23 years for the Irish army. Names lighted on the list and within hours the page was full. Some applied to show that they were interested in travelling but knowing they hadn't got a prayer of going, nor indeed did it suit them to land a tour at that point.

But it stood to your favour in the selection process if it was seen by your superiors that you were applying for every trip. It meant there was an eager intent to serve.

After two years of putting my name forward without success, I got pissed off and went to see my CO, or Commanding Officer. A.J. Mullowney was a tough, sometimes uncompromising officer, who always tried to be fair. When I climbed the stairs to the MP School I met Sergeant John Reid and asked him if the Commandant was around. He looked at me for a second and I think it was in his mind to advise me not to see him.

'He's in the far office,' he says.

'Is he in good form?'

I climbed two-steps. He says, 'Murt?'

'Yeah,' I say, half-turning.

'He's off the fags ...'

Shit.

When I knocked a gruff voice the far side said, 'Come in.'

A.J. was a stickler for rules and very much into soldiering. I thought he believed that soldiers weren't being taught enough about the fundamentals of shooting, and in his time had set about remedying this in the Depot MPC. His instructors, one of which I was later to become, spent a lot of time on the ranges, applying the techniques and coaching others in the doctrine. He was one of a couple of forward thinking officers around who wanted to overhaul the image and professionalism of the Military Police unit, and their success, I suppose, can be measured against the frequent requests the UN made to the Irish government to provide Military Police units for Lebanon, Iraq, Cyprus, Bosnia, Eritrea, Liberia ... so much so that the requests could not always be granted owing to manpower shortage.

He sat in his chair behind his desk, its surface arrayed with blue-backed training manuals. Steam rose from a green-rimmed mug by his elbow. Pens stood in a glass holder like porcupine quills. A half-finished cigarette with a black face sat in the rim of a glass ashtray—a sign that A.J. had lost and then mustered his resolve.

'Well, how can I help you?'

I told him I wanted to serve abroad, that I'd been applying for overseas duty for a long time, and asked if he thought I might ever get my chance. He looked at me, his right eyebrow lifting a little. Questioning. Then he glanced to his left, out the window, pinched his nostrils, fixed his eyes on mine and said he would look at the list and get back to me. I saluted and left, content that I had done all that I could within my own limited power to obtain a trip. Many officers would have listened to the request, said their piece to humour me, and done fuck-all else about it.

Call it jumping the queue, or an attempt to do so. I was letting it be known that I was discontented about the lack of opportunity to serve abroad. Ironically, within a decade, tours of duty were being thrown about like lollipops from a parade float, with never enough hands up for the grab. £150,991

Weeks trickled by and the list was taken down, names selected and sent to the Provost Marshal's office in McKee Barracks, Army HQ, for his consideration. Each command would receive an allotment of places in the forthcoming battalion, for example: five to Western Command, four to the Curragh Command, three to the Southern Command and six to the Eastern Command. With each mission the figures would be re-jigged to ensure a pattern of equality was seen to be at play.

What determined the choice of selection only God knows. All decisions were dependant on the present incumbent PM— Provost Marshal—and his view on matters. Like everything else in Irish society, I expect there was major jockeying for position.

A whisper broke from the orderly room, and spread throughout the unit like furze on fire that the Curragh had been allotted five places. No names, though … but people were sizing up their prospects.

On a unit training day the lecture hall was packed. It was shortly after tea-break. The sun shone. Shadows of steel bars on the outside of the windows stretched across desks and brown linoleum. Steel cannonball holders, glossy black and now used as turf-bins were sad relics of a bygone age. Dust motes danced in oblong shafts of light. Glass warm on the faces of old probationer courses fixed to the walls.

When the names of the successful overseas candidates were announced, my ears had to do a double-take: I had been selected. I was travelling to Naqoura, UNIFIL HQ, to work in a multinational Military Police force. Beside the beach, I was told.

'Poxy bastard,' someone says.

'Jesus, you didn't get the Hills,' says another. 'First-timers always get sent to the hills.'

Weeks later I was due to commence my first overseas orientation course. In the meantime there were jabs to be had, documentation to be prepared, kit to be drawn and tailored, money to be saved and changed into US Dollars, enough to tide you over till the first draw down of credits and per diem pay. Oh, and a will to be made.

The thought of saying goodbye to my wife and son had begun to linger in my mind. Colin, my son, was three years old and I would be away for Christmas and the New Year. In March my fifth wedding anniversary would also swing round. I thought about the things I'd miss out on …

To smother the negativity, I dwelt on the advantages of the extra money. New windows were needed to keep out the Curragh chill and stem the dirty smell of burning from a factory, and an extension suddenly didn't seem such a remote possibility. Besides, half the country appeared to be in transit.

These were bleak days. Three of my brothers had left for the States to find work and the opportunity to earn a decent living. Friends with whom I played soccer had also headed for foreign fields, in many cases only ever to return home on holiday. There was also a guilt issue around the fact that I wanted to leave my family and take in this fresh experience. This would be a parallel life. New feelings and emotions. Change.

But I was mature, 28, interested in keeping fit, a social drinker, and did not have a herd mentality. Pub life and the drink culture irritated me—I'd no sooner arrive in a pub than I'd get an urge to leave again. Unusual for a soldier who by the very nature of his profession has to live within close proximity of his colleagues, the mess being an integral part of army life.

10 Sep. *Diary entry:* The Operations Officer arrives in class today and tells us a little about the history and situation in Lebanon. He says that a PLO (Palestinian Liberation Organisation) group came ashore in Israel from South Lebanon and hijacked a bus on the Haifa/Tel Aviv Road, killing 37 and wounding 76 Israelis. In response, on 15 March 1978, the IDF, Israeli Defence Forces, invaded South Lebanon with some 30,000 troops. As a result Lebanon's Government protested to the United Nations, citing it was not responsible for the presence of Palestinian bases in South Lebanon and had no involvement with the operations of PLO commandos.

The IDF withdrawal was partial, maintaining a strip of land, a buffer zone, to protect its northern territories from guerrilla attack. This buffer zone, the officer says, is called the Enclave. UNIFIL was formed and the multi-national force was, under UN Resolution 425, to confirm the Israeli withdrawal from Lebanon, restore international peace and security, and assist the Lebanese Government regain effective control in the area.

Irish involvement commenced on 12 May 1978. Amal,

Hope, he says, the Shia militia, are the force in power (Sep 1985).
The Palestinians are restricted to refugee camps ...

And so I was soon to start the first of my five tours. These
experiences were to shape me as a person; teach me about other
cultures; give me great joy and sorrow; cause for celebration,
reasons for regret, and unspecified angst.

CHAPTER 2

The evening before I left for Lebanon was a strange one. My shaving gear sat on the draining board, along with a small travel bag of chocolates and books given to me by my parents, to whom I had said my goodbyes earlier that day. There was something surreal in the air, the atmosphere fragile, heightened with expectancy, perhaps caused by the long goodbye, for that was what it was; a yawning goodbye. From July to October—me waiting to go, my wife Bernadette for me to be gone. My son Colin was too young to be aware that he wouldn't be seeing his father for six months. The waiting in itself was a test of endurance. In such a prolonged time-phase the mind, naturally enough, toys with all sorts of notions. There were times that I looked at Colin as he pushed his *Dinky* cars about on the carpet and wondered if and how my absence would affect him. But I loved the army, wanted it as a career and felt inwardly compelled to go, but often I was torn inside and very undecided. I remember the night before I left. Bernadette had gone upstairs to check on Colin, I sipped at a coffee. Benny Hill was on TV. Canned laughter broken by the rapid fall of feet down the stairs. 'There's a mouse,' Bernadette said, 'in our bedroom.'

I used to hate rodents; feared them as much I feared heights.

A natural born coward when it came to those things. There was something ironic I suppose in the fact that a little thing like a mouse unsettled me more than the notion of heading off to a war zone and putting my life on the line. So, I went on a poor quality search.

Back in the sitting room, I said, 'I didn't see a mouse. You're sure you saw one?'

This earned me a withering look.

'You're not going out of here until it's caught.'

'We can sleep in the spare room.'

'Catch it.'

Mid-way up the stairs the mouse scudded past me, into the hall and down into the kitchen. I froze solid. Lock-kneed. My heart had crawled into my mouth as though it had come under fire and wanted to look out and see from which direction.

'Jesus, Murt, move, will you …'

In the end, the mouse darted to freedom through the opened back door.

We walked to the train station the next morning. I wore my khaki uniform and blue beret, carried a green combat jacket over arm. Bernadette pushed Colin in his buggy. It had a dodgy front wheel that squeaked even when oiled. It was a bright morning, not cold, though the station itself was freezing. A sharp breeze blew through the tunnel, in from the Curragh plains, carrying a scent of rain, of furze, the combings of mountain heather. It stole the tears from our eyes that we'd been trying to keep bagged. Bernadette handed me a St Martin relic. I had a dozen others given to me by family, including a prayer said to have come down from Crusader times; the saying of it guaranteed you three days notice of your death! So, there I was, armed with novenas and holy medals to keep me safe, and a Crusader novena that would give me notice of death—dead man walking. I never breathed a word of it—not wanting three-days notice, thank you very much. I don't want to know when I'll die because I can do absolutely nothing about it. The train pulled away, the wrenching slowly done ... the pain of parting, bittersweet. Yet, in the minutes afterwards, there was a pure release. At last it had happened and we could get on with things. We were out of Limbo.

Around the corner from Heuston Station was the now defunct Clancy Barracks, our form-up point. We were due to leave for Dublin airport sometime late in the night. We killed time by hanging round the mess, going to mass, queuing to get the last of our inoculations; Gamma globulin. Swapping stories, making calls home. Travelling with me from the Depot MPC, Curragh Command were CSM (Company Sergeant Major) Mossy Whelan, CS Christy Coyne (The Bear), Corporals Mick Nolan and John Hamill. Mossy was the Company Sergeant Major of the multi-national police force, Christy its Crime Reader.

Beirut's airport was closed because of the war. We were flying to Israel and travelling in military convoy to the Israeli border crossing with Lebanon at Roshaniqra. I remember the anxiety in the terminal as we awaited the call to board the plane. Gathered about in groups, wearing combat jackets because of the chill of that October night – I was excited, looking forward to the tour of duty. It was better than factory life, than humdrum barrack existence. This was adventure, career-building.

***

In the morning the Boeing 737 broke cloud cover and began its descent to the runway at Ben Gurion airport. The soldiers due to rotate home were gathered on a grass strip, all tanned and shedding their greens for their khakis in the backs of open-topped trucks. Guys teased the new arrivals, singing *Jingle Bells*—rubbing in the fact that we wouldn't be home for Christmas. This was it? Israel.

We climbed on to the backs of the white trucks. The convoy eased from the airport on to roads, devoid of potholes. Hebrew shop signs; roads to places I'd read and heard of down the years: Jerusalem, Nazareth. In primary school I'd worked on a project of the world's cities—Haifa was one them. City of Oranges. First impressions were of the broiling sun, the shop signs in Hebrew, the good roads, all in marked contrast to home. I thought of my family, how I was now two hours ahead of them, that they wouldn't be waking for another while. And of how it was a new experience for them to be without me, and for me to be without them. I pushed the lump in my throat away with slugs of warm bottled water and forced my mind elsewhere—did I pack my army issue sunglasses ..? Somewhere along the route, during a break in the journey, I was taken in a Passat and dropped off at a junction to act as a pointsman further down the route for the convoy, directing them. And there I stood, basking in October sunshine, under a road sign that pointed the route more effectively than I could ever manage. After the convoy had passed through my position, the air for moments poisoned by billowing diesel fumes, I was picked up. We drove past Akko, and Nahariya, places I would come to know well, and up the steadily climbing road to Roshaniqra.

Naqoura, UNIFIL Headquarters, is situated about 6 km from the border crossing. It is an enclosed camp beside the sea, a long narrow strip that quartered Swedmedcoy, the UN Hospital, MP Coy, Camp Shamrock, Swedlog (logistics), the French guard, Italair (helicopter wing), civilian and administration offices, transport. Beyond the large t-shaped concrete walls lay Mingi Street, a sinuous row of corrugated shops, bars, and restaurants that catered to the needs of the UN soldier.

The convoy rolled down the coastal road, entered the compound and carried on to Camp Shamrock; those bound for the hills in the morning were billeted in a transit camp. We were accommodated in MP Coy, sharing a room with Finnish MPs. At rotation time there was a doubling up in most rooms, primarily because of an overlap between MPs ending and beginning their tours of duty. Equipment and ongoing investigations needed to be handed over. MP Company had a duty room and cells, Quartermaster's stores, Transport office, Admin block, accommodation prefabs, Special Investigation offices, Traffic Section, a volleyball court, shower area, club and TV room that looked down upon the stony beach and a u-shaped pool bombed into being by French engineers. Meals were provided in the International Mess, not far from the officers' accommodation wings. I was handed a glass of Russian vodka by a Finnish MP in his billet, and sipped at it, then searched for sleep, finding it quickly.

In the silence of the night when sleep was interrupted, there was the noise of the sea, the smell of salt in the air, the stir of clothes on lines, the singing of a song competing against a harmonica ... noises that would die. But never dead was the drone of Israeli patrol vessels that sailed up and down the waters, not far offshore.

The first morning in the shower room, a Norwegian called Od Bernstein, a barrel-chested, gregarious individual, said, 'Keep the hot water running in the sink, yes, because,' he pulled a face, motioning his eyebrows to a Nepalese, 'people wash their feet and their clothes in the bowl.'

***

After breakfast we attended the briefings and went to the stores for our clothing: jungle greens, *Heli Hansen* wet gear, MP brassards, white letters on black. I was to begin work in the Traffic Section and was to report to Gendarme Black in the afternoon. Laminated ID cards and meal vouchers were issued—those with drivers licences had to be tested by a civilian UN field service officer. This didn't concern me as I couldn't drive at the time—I suppose it was an oddity to have someone in the Traffic Section who would be conducting speed checks and investigating traffic accidents, who was a non-driver. Then again, all armies are full of anomalies.

Gendarme Black was a slight man with glasses and jet black hair, a bit of a Dustin Hoffman look-a-like. Our role was mainly to collate the accidents that came in to us from the contingent Military Police in the area of operations, i.e. in the 20 km radius of hills around us. Nations contributing troops were each assigned an area of responsibility and were known as: Fijibatt, Nepbatt, Irishbatt, Ghanbatt, Finbatt, Frenchbatt, Norbatt ...

UNIFIL ran on paperwork; paper, its blood. When a file ended up on my desk, I went to the board on the wall and marked the date it arrived in the office. I then checked the contents page, read the statements, examined the sketch and determined if it concurred with the investigating Military Police officer or NCO when it came to apportioning responsibility for the cause of the accident; if there were mitigating factors, and if the witness statements and evidence tallied with what actually happened. As you can imagine, among a multi-national force, English created a problem, which was the reason an Irish MP proved a vital asset in the Traffic Section, driver or non-driver. It was he who usually made sense of a report and worded it correctly. Gems of this ilk were frequently submitted:

'The wall came up to meet me.'

'I went back into the car which had come out of nowhere and wasn't there when I checked in the mirror.'

'The child ran out in front me and hit my car on the bumper.'

I mention these as examples and not to ridicule—indeed, the English put together by these drivers and passengers was much more coherent than I could have managed if the reports had to be submitted in French or Swedish. Vital pieces of documentation were a photo album and a sketch. Photo albums comprised of pages that held two or three Polaroid shots of the accident. All of this detail was needed in order for civilians in the finance branch to assess claims. It was rumoured that irrespective of blame, the claimant was always paid. What the final report served to guard against was a multiplicity of claims made by the same individual. It does well to remember that there was no police force in Lebanon at this juncture; the gendarmerie had stood down, the country's soldiers remained in barracks, anarchy ruled and the country was lawless—many militia vied for power.

That time in 1985 the *Amal* (Arabic for Hope) militia was in the ascendancy, carrying the fight to the Israelis in the wake of the Israeli invasion and withdrawal. The Palestinian fighters had gone, their power base lost. The MPs were meanwhile busy in the investigation of traffic accidents, drawing upon what he had been taught in the classroom and on the ground, and putting it to good effect. Documentation, the completion of speed check reports and the like didn't faze me. The language had been a blessing in peacekeeping missions as it's a world language. The Irish language, I found, was a curio for the Lebanese and other nationalities. They liked to hear it spoken, the Lebanese quick to pick up on phrases and use them when greeting Irish soldiers.

The Military Police Corp always held an attraction for me. Depot MPC in the Curragh was a small unit and had the look of a family feel to it – there appeared to be a variety of work within the corp that didn't exist in infantry units. A ban on promotion and recruitment was in effect – but the promotion prohibition did not affect the MP corp, and for someone like myself, who was career conscious, it made the corp an attractive proposition. In addition my grandfather had served in the army as an MP.

***

19 Oct: *Diary entry*: It's a pain to listen to the other nationalities converse in front of me in their native tongue – rude, bloody ignorant – Jesus wouldn't I love to be able to give them a dose of their own medicine; hold a conversation in fluid Irish with one of the guys … just to see the look on the bloody faces of the Swedes. Have them wondering what was being said.

★★★

I settled quickly into the 7am to 3pm routine. After normal duty, extra hours kicked round twice weekly and required me to be on call round the clock. The DCO, Deputy Commanding Officer, was Commandant John Meenan from the Curragh, the CO a Norwegian. These were the men in charge of the company. Captain Peter Walsh also from the Curragh, was the company's Admin officer. He was an energetic character, friendly and outgoing, liked to play chess and practise his French with the French MPs. He was killed in a car accident a few years later. A character in the unit was the late Ollie O'Flaherty from Dublin, who had a humorous take on life, wore a little black moustache and regulation short black hair, so you can imagine the Hitler resemblance. How he was never set upon in Israel was a mystery. He smoked too much and liked a drink. I shared a prefab billet with four other corporals but in practice there was only one or two of us staying in it at any given time. My colleague Mick Nolan had gone on detachment to UNIFIL House in Beirut for two months, and Phil Quirke had gone to Tel Aviv MP Detachment, John Hamill to Nahariya, a German-built town about 15 minutes drive from the border. These detachments served to break up the tour of duty, brought you extra money, and gave you new experiences.

Every morning the helicopters began to whirr in Italair, drifting right across MP Coy, over the Moorish keep in the Muslim cemetery and out to sea. The road to Beirut was closed, unsafe to travel and the old Hueys rattled their blades up the coast, staying offshore for the 30 minutes it took to travel. Helicopters had been shot at before and downed, losing all aboard. The full settling into the trip didn't occur until the last rotation had taken place and we weren't under the eye of the outgoing section. There was a relief at seeing the back of them. I was starting to settle, but I was still far from sure how things were going to pan out.

***

27 Oct: *Diary entry:* Sunday. Off duty. Wrote letters home, received none in the post. It's a kick in the arse when the letters are being distributed and there's none there for you. One of the lads says I can read his. Mossy says I'll probably get a load of them together. The letters have stale dates anyway, probably written the day after we left Ireland. I read the newspapers, listen to the BBC World Service, and light a mosquito coil, watch it burn to ash. Read Sherlock Holmes because there is fucking nothing else to read. Think about what prompted me to join the Military Police—did I make the right decision? I never saw myself as someone who could be a PA. Polini Airm, army police, dealing with soldiers and civilians regarding discipline and investigating crime and the like—sometimes I feel uncomfortable around

people and come across as standoffish—wonder why that is? Sometimes it feels like I'm wearing the wrong hat. Jesus, missing home, Bernadette, Colin, family … the food's shite …

CHAPTER 3

Mossy, the Major, told me as we strolled together down the sweep of hill that ran into Camp Martin (named after an Irish MP who had died from natural causes while serving with the company) that I was going to Tyre on detachment for a little over two months.

'What do you think of that?' he added.

Mossy smoked a pipe, burning Clan tobacco which was available in the Swedish PX in the UN Hospital and in a couple of shops along Mingi Street.

He looked into his pipe's chimney and frowned as he said, 'It's not so bad ...'

'No, I'll be fine.'

He turned to me and said, 'I was talking about the tobacco— it's not stale.'

Tyre wasn't a popular choice for a detachment posting. The section was situated in Hassan Burro Barracks, a Lebanese army barracks, on the outskirts of Tyre. Toilet and shower facilities were archaic and you were away from the hub of things, often trapped in barracks because the port city was out of bounds if tensions were running high there. While serving in these outposts Military Police received a daily allowance of $24, called, *Food*

Money, which brought the green goddess to the hearts of non-MPs. The payment was introduced because it wasn't possible for UNIFIL to ensure a constant and regular supply of rations to their personnel in Tyre and Beirut. Later, years later, when the situation calmed, food and cooks were brought on stream and the allowance was terminated, except for detachments in Israel, as Israeli customs would not permit foodstuffs to be brought across the border.

Mossy took it upon himself to bring the Leb first-timers on familiarisation trips throughout the Area of Operations, visiting all of the different Contingent HQs. His knowledge gleaned from his previous tours of duty to Lebanon was invaluable to us, and he wasn't restrictive in what he passed on.

***

My first day went as follows: I kitted up in my green flak jacket and armed myself with a Browning pistol drawn from the duty room armoury, where MPs of all nationalities house separate weapon lockers. The Duty NCO signed me out and for the duration of my journey I had to maintain radio contact with him, MP Control, which he logged in the daily unit journal. Occasionally, armed elements hijack UNIFIL vehicles or fire at them, so it was important in the event of an incident that your exact location was known or could be logically assessed from the point and time of your last transmission.

I then drove along the coastal road, some 6 to 8km from Naqoura, to a road checkpoint manned by the South Lebanese Army, the proxy force trained and paid by the Israel Defence

Force. This Israeli-created buffer zone on Lebanese soil was a false border to deter, pre-empt and thus nullify guerrilla attacks and attempted incursions into Israel proper. The idea being to keep their citizens at arm's length from their enemies. In addition, an electrified fence with fine gravel between fences to determine enemy infiltration was erected along the Israeli 'real' border. To entice recruits into their militia, special inducements were offered: free education, health, family members allowed to work in Israel ... when these weren't enough, conscription occurred. It wasn't unheard of for a young man to be coerced or manipulated by his family into joining the SLA. It also wasn't unknown for a sensitive young man to turn his rifle on himself.

After passing the SLA checkpoint, under the watchful eye of a gunner seated on the turret of a grey Sherman tank, a process of swinging open and closed four long candy striped barriers set at intervals the length of the position, I edged towards the first UN checkpoint manned by Fijians and yet another boom, UN this time. Along the route was a dent in the road where a young woman had blown herself and her mule to smithereens in a failed effort to kill SLA members.

The Fiji checkpoint I pass, after producing my UNIFIL ID card, would in the future be the scene of another bombing incident; a suicide bomber blowing himself up in his car, killing five Fijian soldiers.

The Fijian soldiers shouted, 'Bula, Bula,' a traditional Fijian greeting, whenever I passed, slapping their hands in salute against the butt stocks of their FN rifles. Kilometres on, swinging right, off the coastal road to Tyre, engaging the Burma Road as I passed thorns of Christ growing on the verges, I caught the scent of the orange groves, saw women balance baskets of pomegranates on their heads.

The Nepalese soldiers called out, 'Ram-Ram' when I went by. The villages I noticed were strung along the mountain road like poor quality pearls in a necklace. The higher I climbed, the poorer the village, the colder the air. At Quasimodo's Curve, on the steep rise, I glanced left and in the distance far below saw Tyre, the isthmus, the blue of the Mediterranean, its inshore green.

Irishbatt was next, entering Haris, heading towards Al-Yatun. Mingi shops were clustered here and there, a van pulling up at the roadside, wares being shown to soldiers. I noticed that joggers on the Tibnin run were an indication that the operational level was currently low risk.

I checked in with MPs in Gallows Green, a three-storey house on a slight eminence, whose flat rooftop afforded a panoramic view of the hilltop positions of Irishbatt's Hilltop 880 and its twin hill across a slim ravine, the SLA controlled Charlie Compound.

Driving straight on through Tibnin, down the steep and winding road under the Crusader castle, to a bridge and a T-junction, I stopped, alighted from the Chevrolet jeep, paid respects at this checkpoint manned by Irish soldiers.

Taking a left turn I'd breeze through Al-Sultaniyah village, and into Ghanbatt turf. The soldiers at the checkpoints, call out, 'On the ball, Irish.' In a few months time, an order would go out for them to quit saying this, so they started making the sign of a ball as you passed …

Shebea, which is spelt phonetically; is so called because its real name is Tayr Zibna, which means something rude in Ghanaian dialect, and we try not to upset Ghanbatt. Like a lot of things that you hear you have to take this at face value. You can clearly see, as you travel, the locations of fatal traffic accidents, shootings and fire-fights.

You see scraps of Israeli uniforms hanging on phone lines and telegraph poles, their olive hue sun and wind-worn, frayed …

The driver told me when it was time to return, before Charlie Swing-gate closed for the night. On the way back he stopped off in Total and introduce me to Monsour, a mingi-man, from whom he bought a radio cassette on credit and encouraged me to do likewise – it's handy when on detachment … Monsour was missing an arm and most of the fingers of his hand, injured when he opened a parcel bomb delivered to his home by a competitor whom he had undercut in price.

★★★

'Are you right, Murt—we'll make tracks?'

'Sure.'

I had just attended the dogface meeting. Dogface was the name given to all detachment commanders. Probably because they were the ones barked at and who barked back.

Sergeant Tom Power was a seasoned NCO. He wore glasses with black frames, possessed sound common sense and was neither excitable nor easily vexed. Necessary and valuable traits in a detachment environment when the heat came on. He taught me how to drive, and I had plenty of open space in Tyre Barracks and mounds of tyres to cushion the odd collision.

MP Tyre operated from a long colonial type building,

comprising of a duty room, armoury, kitchen and dining area, shower and toilet, stores and TV room. Each MP had his own room in a prefab on a parade square that fronted the disused Senegalese mess. Hassan Burro Barracks was a vast walled-in affair with corner towers occupied by Ghanaian sentries. A trickle of Lebanese troops showed up on parade most mornings, played table soccer the day long and went home in the evenings, leaving a skeleton crew by the main gate. Their CO used to ride a white horse along the beach and weeks after I landed home I read a report of his death in the *Irish Independent*, ambushed on his way to Tyre Army Barracks. His crime? Collaborating with the UN—though one didn't need a reason to kill someone in Lebanon—it was the style of the times. A reason could be thought of after the killing, if needed. Loose minds with hair trigger tempers and easy access to weapons. A doctor was once shot in Tyre for allegedly carrying out an abortion.

The barracks itself was a graveyard for hundreds of tanks abandoned by the Palestinians when the Israelis invaded. A pack of dogs used one as a kennel and their presence in the barracks seemed to be tolerated, in spite of them possessing a vicious streak.

Tyre detachment consisted of Damar Thapa; Nepal; Joe Cavaluba; Fiji; Capet; France; Od Bernstein; Norway, and Isaac Agyemang; Ghana. Ranks varied from Lance Corporal to Gendarme. Personnel usually ended up spending 70 days on detachment.

Our tasks were varied. The duty NCO manned the duty room, logging the unit journal, ensuring the shower and toilet were clean, taking in weapons from UNIFIL troops on their way to

Tyre to visit the extensive Phoenician ruins in the city by the sea, facing south. The Roman hippodrome, its spectator rostrums, and the Byzantine City of the Dead were situated at the rear of the barracks and used as a training base for young recruits, teens and younger, by the Amal, and was out of bounds to all and sundry—chariot scenes in the film *Ben Hur* were recorded here, and Roman murals had been left on walls in garages within the barracks. Weapons confiscated from armed elements, AE's, by UNIFIL battalions were brought to MP Tyre and secured in an armoury. These were returned to the AE when he presented himself to the detachment. Swings and roundabouts – it made it easier for an AE to hand over his weapon if he knew he was going to have it returned.

My first day in the duty room and Capet walked by the office door carrying a dead rat by its tail. He had removed it from a trap in the kitchen … He smiled at me as though to say, 'Get used to it.'

Capet was thin and tall, balding. He believed that travelling fast along shell-marked roads negated a bouncing action. The duty NCO of the day prepared the evening meal most evenings. We usually dined in whenever Tom or Capet were cooking, but as for the rest of us, the poor fare was enough to decide the detachment would go in relays to town and dine out; not an expensive option. We usually ate in a corner restaurant on the main street, opposite the *Basra* Video Store where we had an account. Chicken and chips the staple and most trustworthy of diets. The owner liked to talk to us about the 'Boom, boom,' that went on in the hills and tell us that the Israelis were no good, saying it as though it were a mantra. Another place we used to dine in was a fish restaurant right by the sea in the Maronite Christian sector, close to the house of an antique and jewellery dealer whose shop was at the top of a narrow passage in the souk. Italian gold was all the rage back then amongst UNIFIL troops, along with handmade suits tailored by Yousef. The fish restaurant was put off limits after Freddie Michon, Capet's replacement, argued with the owner about his raising the prices on each of our visits. Freddie was skinny, had a handlebar moustache and was into martial arts and kung fu films. He monitored the mini-bar chit-list back at the club with a fine eye.

★★★

Even when we tried to make things as much like home as we could, there were always stark reminders that this was not like any other place on earth. Boy soldiers from the Amal militia roamed the darkened streets at night, either carrying RPGs or Kalashnikov rifles. At their checkpoints in and out of the city they'd always ask you for uniforms or boots, using sign language and smiles.

In their camp in the hippodrome, the boys were quartered under the ancient rostrums and if the weather was fine sat on Roman pillars and plinths to eat their meals. I suspect the boys were war orphans: What they most definitely were, was cannon fodder.

Tyre was not an easy posting. Ongoing during my period there was an investigation conducted by the UN to locate a missing Irish soldier. This soldier went missing from a two-man post. His colleague was killed. One of the theories is that the soldiers were caught off-guard by Palestinians, the surviving soldier brought to a cave near Sidon where he was killed by bombs dropped from Israeli warplanes.

Though an FN rifle was found and believed to be his, this was later disproved—it belonged to a Nepalese soldier. A wanted poster was fixed to a wall in the duty room, for a gunman called Barzi who'd allegedly killed two Irish soldiers and wounded another; his face recently appeared on Irish TV, showing him living his new life in the States.

In Tyre, foot patrols were usually done for three reasons: to show an MP presence, to shop, and simply to get a break from the detachment's claustrophobia-inducing conditions. Tyre had been battered during the war, its seafront buildings were shell-shattered, leaving whole rooms visible, some still inhabited. Ships were rusting tombstones in the bay, the sun danced on the glossy carcasses of dogs left to rot on the beach, barefooted kids kicked dead rats about ... you get to see more on a foot patrol... the world you live in falls under the microscope.

Khalil, a fuzzy haired man, frequented the detachment, and he was sort of a Mr Fixit, keeping us abreast of what was happening in town. He was also a sort of an unofficial tour guide. He sold old coins and jewellery he dived for in the sea, taking the crust off by putting them in an acid based solution. His brother who was a dentist fashioned the better pieces into items of much sought after jewellery. Khalil, I later learned, in peace-time—by that I mean after the reunification of Lebanon—became a curator of the Roman hippodrome and the City of the Dead.

The occasional morning we had coffee in the *Phoenician Café*. There was a girl there with whom Capet liked to chat. Dark-haired, very pretty, and while there was nothing untoward in Capet's chit-chat, I saw that the owner disliked and was nervous about the fraternization.

Capet was a dedicated soldier who knew the politics of the UN. One night, when following an open top jeep containing French soldiers, he tooted the horn at a young French soldier, motioning him to put on his beret. But one night we came across a French officer who had parked his staff jeep outside a restaurant. Capet spoke to the officer's driver. Although Tyre was out of bounds to UNIFIL personnel after dark, Capet let it pass without taking action or putting in a report. I said nothing, but should have. I was annoyed at the blatant inequality. The problem was this: if Capet had done his job he would have suffered a backlash—the young conscript in the back of the jeep had no backlash attached to him. It's a problem in all facets of life, I suppose, and it makes my blood boil.

***

I got letters from home, read a lot, made diary entries, most of which have been lost due to several house moves, burned and discarded. I settled in. I found some days boring, repetitive, with long hours spent in the duty room, but overall I enjoyed the tour, the strangeness of being in a foreign country, learning new things, meeting new people.

***

13 Nov: *Diary entry*: Isaac the Ghanaian brings my

attention to the gas cooker. A mouse is inside, his paws—if that's what they call mice feet—to the cooker glass. Isaac goes over and switches on the gas, leaves it run. I'm sick and ready to bolt when he pulls down the oven door—no mouse. I wait for a few seconds and then leave, every bit of my skin crawling …

★★★

Things were reasonably quiet in the run-up to Christmas. We'd had a few minor traffic accidents to investigate, speed checks were conducted on the coastal road, and while at night there was the rattling of machine gun fire, more often than not hailing from the Palestinian refugee camp at Al Rashidiyah, a couple of kilometres south of the barracks, nothing much happened that directly impacted on us… that would change after Christmas.

I was settled in and hadn't suffered Tyre belly, diarrhoea, or endured prolonged homesickness pangs. The tour was progressing nicely. I felt at ease in myself, that I was making a contribution on all fronts: helping the family finances, fulfilling an ambition, furthering my career, and broadening my horizons. This wasn't so bad.

CHAPTER 4

25 December, 1985: *Diary entry*: Christmas Day. Wet and miserable. Cheerless. I call home and it's great to hear and speak with Bernadette and Colin, takes a little out of the sting of homesickness. I think of when I was a kid and the effort Mam and Dad put into giving us a good Christmas, of how my father was always home for Christmas, and how I could never say that about myself. It's only one day, isn't it—one day and Jesus, like, it's the land where Jesus walked. I should be grateful. Like, you know? To be here.

★★★

In the club, Od rose the Norwegian flag above the Irish on the dartboard. He brags about the pocket knife his Government sent to each of its soldiers in Lebanon. He was a police officer in Norway and sometimes he speaks of the bodies he had to pull from cars and of the dead homeless, and the state of despair of the poor unfortunates. He has a habit of tweaking the end of his moustache as though he is winding his lips up prior to winding you up. He is impulsive, generous, and a lot more thin-skinned than he wants us to think.

I hit the bull, a fluke and he's hopping—when it's his turn to throw he fires the darts at the board like they are javelins. We're useless at darts. Even Damar who'd never held a dart in his life before he came to Tyre, can beat us. We're here, the two of us, neither wanting to be alone on Christmas morning, but some others do—they handle being alone at Christmas by staying on their own.

The dinner went well, the evening wore on. Capet retired early, depressed at being away from home, tipsy with red wine. We had blue barrels of the stuff in the store room. Damar sat idly by—non-vegetarian for the day. Joe the Fijian stayed in the Duty room, Isaac went to his brother Ghanaians in their dining hall. Od got into a row with a Swedish OGL (Observer Group Lebanon) officer, two of whom were stationed in Tyre Barracks and kept pretty much to themselves. Od insisted on inviting them over for dinner in spite of the fact that it was they who'd wanted nothing to do with us and not vice-versa—an officer and other rank thing. When it was time to quit on the night, Od rushed to the door. He was unsteady and flustered, and pulled on the doorknob. The door wouldn't budge. He tugged again, a mystified look on his face.

'What the fuck is this? Are we locked in? Who locked us in?'

'Od,' Tom said drily, 'take your toe from the door.'

'Oh, fuck,' Od said.

Sound advice.

***

I was last to bed, remaining on to polish off a beer, not retiring till the last of the kerosene ran out in the red heater, sighing a black puff, its globe wires losing their glow … the scratching of a rat out back. Maybe not, but the notion was strong enough to drive me from the loneliness of the club to the loneliness of the billet. Thank God for the cassette radio and the BBC World Service.

I lit a candle on my billet table, read a few pages of a book I'd bought about Tyre. I had this urge to know the bones of the place I was staying in. Tyre is one of the oldest cities in the world, mentioned in the Bible many times—its Phoenician ruins are impressive with its colonnaded avenue to the sea, its mosaic flooring, sarcophagi, Roman amphitheatre—so many dead worlds dug out by trowel and sweat: Phoenician, Greek … Roman. So much lost, stolen—people used the columns and fine stonework as foundations for their houses, other items discovered were channelled into the black market. Tyre was originally an island, its topography changed by Alexander the Great when he constructed an isthmus and breached the city's formidable walls, crucified the inhabitants along the new causeway as punishment for delaying his military campaign. I thought too of our drive to the hippodrome a few days before, with Isaac at the wheel, carrying live shells in ammunition boxes filled with sand on the bed of the jeep. The sand was to prevent the shells from being jarred into exploding by the jeep's motion over shell marked roads. Irishbatt Military Police had brought us this ordnance. Amal youngsters removed the shells and started shaking and slapping them. At that very moment Israeli warplanes flew low over the city on their way north.

'Maybe we all die today,' the boy said, with zeal and hopeful expectation in his eyes.

Like, get me the fuck out of here, I thought. Isaac was already revving dirt.

The man in charge of the boys, Abou Harb, emerged from the side of the rostrum, issuing instructions, initiating the scheme of defence. He paid us no heed. We drove on through the city, the streets lined with people scanning the skies, the silence, given the crowds was surreal, like something from a scene in a sci-fi movie. It was as though their eyes were waiting ... the fear in them all too palpable.

I started a letter to home but crumpled the paper and went to bed. I was tired and a little bit ashamed of the fear I had felt in the hippodrome, how the blood in me had run cold, in comparison to the young fighter who'd relished the prospects of action. There were things you didn't write home about; the fear was one, the loneliness another; you didn't want to worry people. There were things I wanted to express, but couldn't, and not in a letter home—not that night—my heart wouldn't let me hold the pen. I guess I was disappointed with myself, at the way my knees had turned watery when the warplanes flew overhead. I thought of the boys in the hippodrome and how they'd no future and how the lack of one did not appear to unduly concern them.

***

Days into the New Year, 1986, I was returning from collecting traffic accident photographs from the camera shop outside the barracks, when Isaac called me into the office.

'Something has happened in the AO—you must go and investigate. A bad accident.'

Tom was away in Naqoura with Damar. Od was already zipping up his flak jacket, while Joe was turning the key in the armoury door. Isaac went outside to hear better and answer a call on the Motorola, while I rang MP Control. It was engaged.

Isaac returned and said, 'In Nepbatt, Kafra village ...'

We loaded up our traffic accident box, checked the camera for film, and left the barracks, travelling the coastal road towards Naqoura. The MP Duty NCO came over the radio and gave us precise details, '... proceed with caution.'

Od looked at me, his voice cracking, 'What the fuck did he say, Murt?'

'Proceed with caution. Take care.'

His cheeks and throat flamed. Now and then his fingers lighted on the handle of his Luger pistol, as though it were a holy relic, something from which he might draw comfort.

Travelling the mountain road to Kafra I wondered what lay ahead of us. The villages along the way were quiet, almost deserted. Kafra village was close to the Irishbatt village of Haris and lay about half a mile from the main road, accessed by a thin lick of rutted asphalt. The air was tainted by the after silence of a bad happening. The UN flag pole on the roof of the Nepalese position lay broken, the flag draped across a veranda, its corner giving a limp wave in the mountain breeze.

A Nepalese officer guided us to the scene of the carnage; a tiny square with a gnarled olive tree guarded by a railing. Irish soldiers had made the call in. They had been in Gallows Green, MP Irishbatt, when the news came over the radio. One was standing on a rooftop photographing the scene. Od left and Joe stood alongside me, waiting to be told what to do. It was carnage, a horrifying scene, and we had to walk right into it. There was blood on the walls, a severed hand by the olive tree close to a black ammo magazine and 7.62 rounds lying on the ground, torn from a soldier's rifle. In front of me lay a woman's foot with a blue legging. A marmalade cat darted along a wall, feeding on flesh. What were we supposed to do here? All I could think of were the practicalities. We put the hand and the foot into a black bag and carried on with the investigation.

As it turned out, Amal guerrillas had attacked an SLA compound overlooking the village, and the SLA responded by firing a tank round from its Sherman, which killed an 18 year old woman, her young life cut tragically short. The severed foot was all that was left of her. Nepalese soldiers were on their way to assist the villagers when another round landed, killing one of their men.

Two tank rounds, two deaths. The soldier was a week away from going home … which was exactly where I wanted to be at that moment.

***

We returned home by another route to Tyre. Passing King Hiram's tomb, the Tyrian king who supplied Solomon with materials to build his temple in Jerusalem. There wasn't much conversation in the jeep on the way to barracks—we were relieved to be putting distance between us and Kafra, akin to the feeling you get when you walk out a hospital door after being a patient for a few days.

I went into the duty room and typed up a report, while Od had a couple of beers and talked into the early hours with sentries at the Lebanese gates. A couple of loud echoes of, 'Oh, my God, it was terrible ...' rose above the chirping of cicadas.

Therein lay the key to counselling, he was talking about his experience, filtering it from his system, even if he was unaware he was doing it. I was committing the incident to paper, another sort of filtering.

The scene at Kafra was not a major one in the context of Lebanon's history of war atrocities: two fatalities. Lebanon is less of a country and more of a battleground for other nations. It is a cauldron of festering hatred and ageless enmity, where the innocent are probably five-times more likely to be killed in conflict than a single combatant. I love the land, its ruggedness, its people—it was a home from home for me, and perhaps this love was borne out of sympathy for a war-torn race, a country used as a proxy by Syria and Iran to attack Israel, or perhaps it's just an affair of the heart. If so, it defies explanation.

CHAPTER 5

On my return from Tyre I spent three-weeks performing duties at Roshaniqra border. It was mid-January and the weather was mostly damp and overcast. Strong winds enhanced the smell of salt air, muscled the orange wind sock on the beach to life. I kept writing in my diary, a few lines here and there, leaving pages empty because some days the days were blank. I wrote whenever I felt like it. Perhaps it was in me without my knowing, the seed of an idea to write a book, and I was recording details for future use:

6 Jan: *Diary entry*: As Military Police we are responsible for and tasked with searching the baggage of UN personnel, military and civilian, crossing into Israel. We are monitored by Israeli soldiers who ensure that the checks are properly carried out. In the vehicle hangar across from the terminal an MP oversees an Israeli mechanic as he searches UN vehicles for contraband. A few UN vehicles have clearance to cross the border without undergoing a search—I think this is called diplomatic immunity—restricting the right to smuggle to a privileged few is one jaundiced comment I've heard bandied about. Many UNIFIL vehicles and UN personal cars are parked a little way

from the border, in a lot that is guarded at night by a civilian security guard and visited by Military Police from Nahariya.

Field Service staff in general dislike Military Police, perhaps because they resent their bags being searched, being refused permission to bring this or that item across the border. Field Service, all civilian staff, reside in Nahariya and cross the border to work in the mornings and after work in the afternoon. Today the bus drops them a couple of hundred yards from the border crossing terminal and they have to walk a couple of hundred yards uphill to the building. The Israelis like to discommode people just to prove that they can. A Swedish Field Service officer approaches me at the search counter giving out stink about the bus dropping him off at a distance from the terminal. I wonder what the fuck he wants me to do about it but I remain silent. I have a heart condition, he says. His attitude to me is disrespectful, his tone almost a snarl, eyes cutting. I let him go on for about five minutes, the tirade witnessed by the Israelis. Eventually, he pauses, breathless. I say, mustering as much diffidence into my tone as possible, 'I'm sorry, could you say that again, please—if you wouldn't mind, I didn't quite hear you?'

Some Field Service personnel would have been involved in traffic accidents and other incidents and resented being questioned and having their names mentioned in Military Police reports, perhaps being cited as having contributed to an accident. Military Police in some countries would not have been revered, either—once, a Polish officer brought three Irish MPs into his office and asked them not to beat up his officers! A common thing in Poland, perhaps? Military Police in some parts of the world are used as a dirty tool by their governments … as with the Irish government when they had Military Police guarding civilian prisoners in the Glasshouse at the Curragh—Military Police were a cheaper option than prison officers, and constrained in what they could say to the outside world. The men and women staffing Field Service hailed from every neck of the world, so God knows what practices they brought from home.

I think every MP who served in MP Coy from all nationalities would have stories to tell you about Field Service. What people sometimes forgot was that the Israelis pulled the Military Police up if their searches weren't thoroughly done. Now and then an MP befriended an Israeli soldier and a smuggling racket would commence and endure until either the Israeli or/and the MP was posted elsewhere in the natural course of his duty. Sometimes the arrangement was passed on like a family store, but more often than not the incoming MP and Israeli were 'straight,' and the link was severed, but would begin again down the line. A resurrection if you will. The mules would buy contraband in Mingi Street and bring across goods such as electrical items, watches, jewellery, alcohol, in essence anything that was in demand, in fashion at a given time—it varied. In future trips I was to learn much more about the smuggling rackets and how rife they were throughout UNIFIL, although this was strictly forbidden by the UN.

***

One day, Mossy called me into his office one day and said, 'You're going to Nahariya, to mind the Force Commander's House for a week—he's gone to Ireland—don't use the phone …'

It seemed that someone had once abused the Force Commander's phone and run up a sizeable bill when he'd been away, which he'd obviously queried on his return. The Force Commander at that time was Irish, Brigadier General Bill Callaghan, The Bull Callaghan. He was a soldier's officer —fair, popular, tough, and straight. You knew he cared about the men under his control; he had that aura about him and you were also aware that he would never put a soldier in a situation where he himself would not venture. This in an indefinable and inexplicable quality—it cannot be taught or mimicked—you're either the genuine article or you're not. Lt Gen Callaghan was the longest serving UNIFIL Force Commander and was later awarded the DSM (Distinguished Service Medal) for his display of outstanding leadership in times of great difficulty.

The Force Commander's quarters itself was a bungalow with a large manicured lawn that ran almost to the Akko Road. In the garden was a bomb shelter. The week dragged, with rare visits from Nahariya Military Police. A gardener from Camp Tara in Naqoura called in on Wednesday to mow the lawn, said he used to be an MP, but that he was all right now ...

While I was there, I received phone threats nightly, with people saying they were going to slit my throat. I was aware that someone before me had refused to stay in the bungalow as a result of the threats he had received. But they didn't faze me. Not in the least. In fact whenever my new phone friend called I used to thank him, saying it was fierce lonely and I was glad of the chat—he threatening me and I talking to him. Once he paused when I'd invited him round for a beer ... and he appeared to consider this before saying, 'I'm going to slit your ...'

Diary entry: When the general returns he thanks me and goes to give me a $10 note—I don't want to take it but he isn't someone you say no, to—at least not too easily. Maybe he is pleased that all the calls on his phone are incoming and the contents of his mini-bar are intact. I will hold my hand up to reading a couple of his books, and to sleeping with his sword ...

★★★

The trip moved on. Days grew into weeks. General Callaghan presented the UN medal to MP Coy, Saint Patrick's day slipped by, MP Coy soccer team of which I was captain was beaten 1-0 in the Command Cup Final. The matches were tough and hard fought affairs —the team included Od, Isaac Agyemang, Chris Coyne, and Francis the Fijian, who 13 years later would grab my shoulder in the phone booth in the old OGL lines and squeeze, and for a few minutes talk about where the years had brought us.

That first tour of duty left lasting impressions: a new world had been opened to me, a world where a bright sunny day could be marred in a millisecond, where my uniform in the eyes of some defined me as something, an object of authority and not as a person with rights, too, and that there was one rule for some, and another for everybody else.

★★★

22 April: *Dairy entry*: The night before going home. I drink a can of Al Maza beer in the club and then another. In

the morning we'll roll across the border and join the convoy for Ben Gurion airport. In bed writing this, I think about the trip—Tyre, the shelling and deaths in Kafra, the anger I felt after that incident—the senseless waste of life. The friends I'd made ... the culture of other worlds coming together, the blend rich and invigorating—overall, yeah—I enjoyed the trip. But ... Occasionally a strange lost sort of mood takes me over, my feelings, and though I travel deep inside I never quite find what I'm looking for ... there is that—the angst, too. What good have I done? What did I contribute towards bringing peace to Lebanon? I don't feel as though I have done much and yet by being part of an organisation set up to do good, I am part of that good intention. A cog. UNIFIL has no chance of ever being a successful mission without the co-operation of the warring neighbours. And I don't think this'll be forthcoming, at least not any time soon. I want to get home, be with family, enjoy the month off, spend time with Colin ...

At home, it took me a while to settle down. Things had changed, subtle changes I couldn't quite put a finger to. There was a period of re-adjustment for the family—to get used to each other all over. As with most soldiers on their return from service abroad, I felt a little out of place. In my absence time and people had not stood still ...

CHAPTER 6

A week or so after being told that I had been selected to serve a second term abroad as acting sergeant overseas, in the Hills, my wife Bernadette rapped on the kitchen window—I was in the yard feeding our dog, Trudy, wondering how on earth the neighbour had trained her to chase crows instead of sheep.

'Yeah?' I said, washing my hands, sensing something was up and hoping it wasn't bad news coming.

'I've some news.'

When I heard it I just looked at her, then I said, 'You're sure?'

A nod.

Christ. After a decade …

I was going to be a dad again.

We hugged and smiled through the shock. If you were to ask us on a ratio of one to ten what we thought the future held for us, coming in last would have been this news. We didn't think this was for us; in fact we'd given up on the idea and to be honest it never unduly alarmed or caused us much thought, except when someone trying to make us feel bad in ourselves would breathe, 'Only child, lonely child.'

If it happened, it happened. If it didn't, it didn't … but now it had, and as usual in such cases they seldom occur at the most convenient of times.

We talked at length. I wanted to take my name off the overseas list, but Bernadette suggested otherwise. What good would I do by being at home? I took this to mean that I hadn't been of much use to her when Colin was born, which was true. When all is said and done, the pushing and shoving is done by the woman, and the physical pain and emotional turmoil isn't softened by holding her hand and encouraging her to, 'Push.'

I had found that out with Colin's birth, and to be honest I fancied that Lebanon was a safer place for me than a maternity ward.

I hate to see a man fawning over a woman and vice-versa, so sickeningly sweet it isn't wholesome, at least I don't regard it as being wholesome or in the least bit genuine. But maybe that's just me.

Bernadette had a good family network around her and without that type of support it wouldn't have been possible for me to travel. I was fortunate in that regard. If she had been anyway uncertain, fearful, I wouldn't have travelled. I had first and foremost a commitment to my wife and family, but I had also made a commitment to serve in Lebanon, and it wasn't a question of divided loyalties—we genuinely didn't see the need for me to remain at home.

Looking back at things now from the remoteness of years, I think we made the wrong decision —and I should have been more of a man and scratched my name—but then I was a career soldier and Bernadette was helping me to be that.

I confided in no one, primarily because it wasn't anyone else's business and if I had mentioned it to my superiors, I would have been putting them in a situation where they had to re-consider sending me abroad. People ended up being repatriated from Lebanon for a variety of reasons; bereavements, disciplinary, injured, or at the behest of a wife.

Also, it was not unknown for a soldier to write to his wife and ask her to get him the hell out of Lebanon because his courage had failed him—perhaps he hadn't settled in or a round had whizzed by his ear, or he'd seen a comrade or civilian blown to bits ... maybe he'd had a premonition and simply acted on it. Usually, however, it was his spouse who set the wheels turning—she simply couldn't manage at home without him, and perhaps hadn't even wanted him to travel abroad to begin with.

Prior to travelling overseas the soldier undergoes an Orientation Course designed to train and prepare him for service in Lebanon. In time, to the old hats who had high numerals on their UN ribbons, this was a fact of army life they saw no real purpose or merit in, and I knew soldiers who, while they didn't mind service abroad, just couldn't face into 'the shit,' that went on before they actually set foot on soil that was no longer foreign or strange to them.

The training for service in the Hills was tougher than it had been for MP Coy. Indeed, Naqoura, UNIFIL Headquarters, was called Swanbatt, because the living there was easy. This was true. There were manoeuvres in the Glen of Imaal; a battle simulation whereby you inserted yourself in a trench and bullets whizzed over your head and bombs detonated nearby while the engineers threw dirt, smoke and loud noise at you. I remember sitting in a trench and seeing officers wearing industrial ear defenders, sitting beside soldiers who had their fingers or tiny tit plugs in their ears.

Most of our training was conducted in Cathal Brugha Barracks with an overnight stay in Kilbride camp, in cramped quarters, because someone thought we should know what the black of the night looked like in the mountains. He was right; the black of the night in the Wicklow mountains looked the same as the black of the night in the Lebanese hills. Dark is dark.

As Military Police we were more or less left to our own devices, but were heavily involved in point duties, and implementing traffic control, via route recce and signing. The battalion comprised approximately 800 troops and ten of these were Military Police, most of whom I would have trained on a probationer's course. Each of the section deserves a mention. Paddy Barrett was the Company Sergeant, CS, an even-tempered, cool-headed NCO, the other sergeant in the Section was Mickey Rall from Cork. The corporals were Alan Walsh, Phil McEntyre, Patsy Walsh, Kevin Murphy, Peter Murphy, Martin Sumner and John Lonergan. The MP officer was Captain Brendan Markey.

The battalion, as with all UN bound battalions, was filtered into Lebanon over three rotations during a three day period and these rotations were referred to as, 'Chalks,'; Chalk I, Chalk II … I was due to fly out on Chalk I, accompanied by Captain Markey, CS Barrett, and Sgt Rall.

Leaving home this time was the hardest of all. Fastened to the back of my mind was the fact that I was leaving behind my wife who was pregnant. Looking back now, I shouldn't have gone … I shouldn't have been let go … Bernadette could have encountered complications and needed me to be with her. What if something went wrong? If something happened in the Leb —I could die never having seen my son's face. My absence wasn't exactly helping to strengthen the marriage ties, either. In fact, if anything, it was loosening them. I should not have left and Bernadette should have insisted that I stay. And fuck the army and letting the side down. But then indulging in hindsight is a fool playing at being wise.

***

It was strange by-passing Naqoura and facing a run of 18 km into the hills. Charlie Swing-gate was still operating, though the Sherman tank was no longer in situ. The roads leading into Irishbatt had been much improved. There were street lights in some villages, though the poverty was still very evident.

The power and the dress code of Military Police in the area of operations differed from those in UNIFIL MP Coy; Military Police in a battalion had responsibility solely for their own area and wore a black brassard with MP in red letters, while UNIFIL MP wore a black brassard with white lettering and had powers of arrest and search that superseded those of Battalion MPs.

On the journey I breathed a short prayer for a colleague of mine, Martin Tynan, who had been due to travel overseas but had failed the medical. Martin passed his overseas medical during the summer and went to Lebanon with the 72 Inf Bn in October of that year. He died in tragic circumstances while on a 60 hour pass in Israel—R.I.P.

There was a meal in the cookhouse at Camp Shamrock and afterwards Irishbatt MPs brought us to Gallows Green. Military

Police were based in a house with a flat roof. The gardens were wild and housed a prefab billet known as *Hell's Kitchen*. Fronting this was the bunker or bomb shelter, covered with rocks similar to those in the gabion nets that flanked the hard tack yard directly in front of the house. The rooms on the ground floor were accessed through a steel door and comprised the Investigator's office, Captain Markey's office, off which was a prison cell, the rear-link room, a radio communications system manned by a signals operator who came up from Camp Shamrock each day, and a store. The second and third floors were accessed via another steel door at the front of the house. The second floor contained our duty room, kitchen, sitting room, bathroom, and two bedrooms. The rooftop had a parapet of sandbags and a corner post, sandbagged, corrugated roof, housing binoculars and 77 radio set for communication with Headquarters and other stations. The view from here was panoramic and was used as a briefing post by officers and NCOs to familiarise others with the topography of the area of operations.

The house was in a general state of disrepair. In winter the water ran down the walls, leaving them black and reeking of dampness. But there were also holes in the walls. The ceilings were paint-flaked. Our nearest neighbour was Normaintcoy, the Norwegian Maintenance Company, which carried out repairs to certain makes and models of UNIFIL vehicle. MPs received damage reports on vehicles involved in accidents from the Norwegian transport office. Their food and dining facilities, PX, were the best in the area of operations, surpassing those in Naqoura. Ours were fairly grim, but it wasn't so bad.

23 April: *Diary entry*: Spent today on familiarisation patrols within the A.O. Haddatha, Tulin, Al-Jurn, Bra-Shit, Haris, Al-Yatun, Tibnin, Al-Sultaniya, Total and other villages. Our interpreter is Hassan Fawaz who lives in Tibnin, on the road to Total. The walls of his home are perforated here and there with bullet holes the size of a man's fist. Millionaire homes presenting easier targets to the Israeli and South Lebanese Army have been left untouched, lending credibility to the rumour that the owners of these palatial homes, many with swimming pools, pay a 'protection fee' to the SLA. Missing home…

Towards the end of the week we stayed overnight in MP Coy, Naqoura, as we were crossing the border in the morning to recce the route for the convoy, Chalk 2, to Ben Gurion airport. I was driving a soft-skinned Peugeot, slow on the hills and not too speedy on the straight stretches either. We got lost outside Tel Aviv and ended up on a beach and had to ask a hooker for directions.

Our section arrived out in dribs and drabs. Many were first-timers and those who weren't hadn't served abroad as Military Police. Brendan Markey was a fine officer, intelligent and put a lot of reason and refined logic into his decisions, and he didn't blow a gasket when things went wrong – he saw a problem and redressed it without creating a fuss. Paddy Barrett was also cut from the same cloth—a problem was a problem, never exaggerated.

Our two Murphys were sizeable fellas with amiable and obliging personalities– one tall, the other short. As such we called them Big Spud and Little Spud. Alan Walsh was probably officer material—he was very solid and clued into what was going on around him. He was awarded a medal for bravery for saving a life in Dublin; something which he never mentioned or spoke of. Phil McEntyre was quiet and hard working. We had an excellent crew and though sometimes there were personality clashes none was ever serious, and the section never stopped working for each other—unlike other sections where internecine feuds ruined trips; horror stories where confined living conditions had got the better of people.

***

We were kept busy on this tour, but I was glad because the investigations took my mind off other matters. The lads were the same—no-one liked staying cooped in the house. My task was to investigate crime that occurred within the Irishbatt area of operations. Along with Brendan, I had been on an investigation course and having passed was thus deemed suitably qualified. I had trained in Garda Headquarters, completed a six to eight week course, as a Scene of Crimes Examiner. It seemed I had a natural aptitude for not taking things at face value. I also investigated and collated traffic reports, my experience in MP Coy standing me in good stead.

Our duties consisted of a two man daily patrol, a Duty Room NCO, one resting, a relief NCO. Not a lot of leeway there when holidays and additional duties came our way—such as escort and convoy duties, and we were also about to be tasked with 'minding' a prisoner who was serving an 18 month sentence for an alleged assault on a woman in Israel. This soldier was being held in a cell in Nahariya MP detachment, but in reality it was more of a house arrest. We would each spend 14 days in Israel, without a detachment allowance. Which was a discrepancy never addressed. I suppose we looked at the fortnight in Nahariya as a respite from the rigours of the AO.

I liked to go on foot patrol and usually dragged someone along with me who didn't want the exercise, because we walked for kilometres, wearing blue flak jackets and carrying loaded Steyr rifles slung over our shoulders. Little Spud was one victim.

No one was really afraid or nervous during these foot patrols because in the initial months of the tour very little fighting took place. But Irishbatt sat right under the intimidating compounds manned by the SLA and Israelis, and though we were living under the sights of someone's firearm, I didn't stop to think about it because my nerves would act up. I put it out of my mind. In spite of the occasional 'stray' round zipping over our jeep …

We walked through the village most days, up by the hospital, the Muslim cemetery, under the honey-coloured walls of the Crusader castle called Castle Turon because of its four stout corner turrets. The walk was long, steep and arduous. At the foot of the castle lay the village waterhole, stagnant, algae-covered. The path that led up the castle arch was narrow and dusty. It was easy to imagine the surviving 13 French knights leaving the castle on their horses, allowed to take nothing with them, their lives spared by Saladin because the knights had previously saved the lives of Muslims from renegades—the credit system of favours …

We broke for lunch in Chicken George's usually. Chicken George's kitchen was an old cargo container – he told us that his son had joined the Lebanese Army and that things were at last looking good for peace in his country. Later, we were greeted in a mingi shop outside the gates of Normaintcoy, Camp Scorpion, by the owner who spoke better Irish than we did!

One day, on return to Gallows Green, Little Spud said, 'Never fuckin' again— the legs are worn to nothing.'

Big Spud said, rubbing his shaven fair hair, 'Did you walk far?'

'About ten miles,' Little Spud said.

'That's nothing, and it has you sweating like a pig ...'

'You try it and see if you're able for it, fat fucker you ...'

'Now lads,' I said.

'I will try it,' Big Spud said, indignantly.

The banter was in no way cruel or demeaning. We were soldiers and friends.

CHAPTER 7

Within a couple of weeks we'd investigated a few traffic accidents—all minor. The finished reports were sent to Traffic Section in MP Coy. There was a theft from a store and a 46 radio set taken from the back of an SISU APC in Al-Yatun. These 46 radio sets are larger, heavier, more cumbersome than their cousin, the 77 set, and are usually found in the rear of Land Rovers—the soldier calls such a vehicle an FFR, Fitted for Radio. The 46 set has a wide range of frequencies and can transmit long distances. The culprit was later identified as a man with one eye who lived in a village near a laundry. We were told to drop the investigation as the person in question was regarded as extremely hostile and rumoured to have shot a man dead in Qana, Fijibatt HQ. It wasn't worth it.

Now and then we dropped down to Naqoura, MP Coy, and stayed for a couple of hours, eating out and buying in what we needed on Mingi Street, catching up on all the news in the MP Club. Tyre had changed; Lebanese gendarmerie were being drilled in the town, the young militia members were no longer in the hippodrome, this patrolled by a caretaker who blew on a whistle at anyone who ventured near areas that were now considered out of bounds.

Likewise with the Phoenician ruins. Lebanon had a Government, elections in the offing—demonstrators burned tyres on the roads in protest at increased taxes, sending black palls of smoke into the air, the stinking smell of burning rubber spreading for miles around.

Hezbollah (Arabic for Party of God) was now the predominant militia in the country – in addition to carrying out attacks against the Israelis, they worked within the community at grassroots level, providing free medical care and food, re-building houses damaged by Israeli artillery. Building a strong support base, all fuelled by Syrian, Iraqi and Iranian money. The first three months of the trip was relatively incident free. Hassan insisted however that once the crops were harvested, trouble was round the corner.

And he was spot on. From the middle of August there was a steady increase in violence. In the spring and summer it was traditional for armed element activity to slacken or cease altogether in order to allow the farmers bring in their crops. The respite afforded the Hezbollah an opportunity to implement new strategies and train up fresh recruits. The Hezbollah used to film their raids for propaganda purposes and air them on Lebanese television.

I went to Nahariya for a fortnight to assume responsibility, prison officer duties, of a soldier who had a charge of sexual assault hanging over him. It was an easy two weeks. The soldier required little looking after, no monitoring. I told him that he was to carry on as he had being doing when the other MPs were with him, and that if he was up to anything untoward I didn't want to know about it. I caught up with my writing and reading, took long walks, had a few beers, enjoyed the late dinners and the bit of craic. Among the MPs in the detachment were Arnie Halvorsen, and Stig, both Norwegian, and Christian, a French MP. Arnie was about 56 and looked like a true Viking warrior; golden locks on the wane, groomed moustache and beard, piercing blue eyes and the manners of a saint. He was a Major in the police in Norway. He brought me to the city of Akko, to the ramparts where across the bay the helium lights of Haifa shimmered on the inshore waters. It was late at night and the city was quiet. Sleeping.

10 July. *Diary entry:* Arnie and I are sitting in a fish restaurant. The restaurant is u-shaped and the tables are seated round the outline of the u, the sea filling the cavity with translucent greens—there's a smell of salt water, of barbecued meat. I'm thinking that Bernadette would like this and of the experiences we've missed out on together. Arnie tells me that he thinks the prisoner has a key to his cell. I'm not too sure why he's telling me this, and what he wants me to do about it, and then I realise he wants only to make me aware of what's going on.

Arnie probably thought I needed to be put wise—I didn't. I was astute enough to realise that the prisoner was caught in no-man's land and that his case in the annals of UNIFIL was unique. In such circumstances you wing it through the grey areas and hope you're doing more good than harm ... I never discussed the prisoner's case with him, asked him if he was guilty. Partly because I felt he'd been asked too many times and was blue in the face from answering, partly because I really wasn't all that interested. Our orders regarding the confinement and treatment of the prisoner were merely cover orders – to appease the Israeli authorities who had reluctantly allowed him to spend his time in UN custody while awaiting trial, and to spare the blushes of the UN authorities should he be discovered by the Israelis, say … sunning himself on the beach, out jogging, etc.

Little Spud and Patsy had come to stay overnight before heading off on leave the next morning. Late at night on his way to his room, Little Spud walked into a bush and was heard muttering and cursing. Over breakfast the next morning, Maria, the Swedish Dogface (the person in charge of the detachment), wasn't behind the door in telling him that he had disturbed her from a sound sleep. He was as sharp as a knife. He adjusted his sombrero and smiled, said it could have been worse.

I enjoyed the two weeks immensely. To be able to walk down the street in civvies and make a phone call home on the spur of the moment was sheer bliss. It was unusual staying in the detachment in the sense that I sometimes expected to see Chris Coyne walk in or one of the other faces from my time there in 1985. I'd thought of the morning when Chris spent 20 minutes showing and telling a Nepalese Sergeant Major the state he expected to find the kitchen in when he returned, the Sergeant Major smiling and nodding and of course six hours later when Chris returned the kitchen hadn't been touched—and all during the subsequent bollocking the Nepalese major smiled and nodded …

Back in the hills I had to deal with an incident in Camp Shamrock. Someone had had his wallet stolen and blamed a young boy who helped in the kitchen, locking him inside a walk-in freezer. I recorded a statement from the aggrieved party who couldn't understand the implications of what he had done. He sincerely believed that the boy had stolen the contents of his wallet, some US $300 and for him that was the real issue, not the locking in. His companion said he had no part to play in locking the boy in the fridge. Years later I was to read a report about him being wanted for questioning by Israeli police, but he had gone missing, presumably back to his country of origin. They were not Irish.

I was annoyed upon learning this—it was frustrating because I'd suspected that he knew a lot more about the theft than he was willing to admit. I also knew the young lad in question—he was very trustworthy. It annoyed me to think that these two men had acted abominably; one who was probably aware of what had happened to his colleague's money and the other for jumping to conclusions. These guys were on a good salary and the boy was, what? Earning a few dollars as a washer-up, a general labourer? The book was judged by the cover, instantly. It was another example of the travesties of justice that happened in Lebanon. In the eyes of the Lebanese boy, well, what did he think of being incarcerated in a walk-in freezer, being blamed in the wrong by the very people there to help him and his country? Did anyone ask him?

***

Meanwhile Hezbollah had been elected to the Lebanese parliament. This would be akin to the IRA taking seats in Leinster House. The celebrations in Tibnin got out of hand— bullets from weapons discharged into the air had landed in Camp

Shamrock and Normaintcoy, causing near misses to personnel and damaging property. An order came through from Ops for the Military Police to report to the gendarmerie station in the village and see if they could do something to address the matter.

The Lebanese gendarmes had a reputation for ineffectiveness, one which, in spite of their country getting back on its feet, hadn't much improved. Big Spud drove our soft-skinned patrol car outside the gates where we waited to sandwich the Peugeot between two APCs. He told me about the UNIFIL Soccer final between Ghanbatt and Irishbatt, how there was a witch doctor and a leprechaun, and the Irish won 1-0 thanks to a penalty awarded by a French referee who had to be protected from the Ghanaians.

'Mayhem,' he said, 'they went fuckin' bananas ...'

All the way down the Tibnin Road, gunfire blitzed the skies, some of it quite close but not dangerously close. In the village the lead APC parked to the right to allow us pass them. The gendarmes inside the rundown station were watching TV— about four of them. Nervous in themselves. When I explained what had happened—one had good English—he nodded and shrugged and spoke in Arabic to a bystander. I understood that he was asking this person to bring someone to him.

About ten minutes later this small man arrived. He had an expensive jacket draped round his shoulders. I extended my hand and he took it up. He was dark-haired, in his early forties and carried an air of authority. In a strong Chicago accent he asked me the problem. He listened intently, nodded and then said something to someone in his small entourage ... that was it. The firing stopped.

***

One huge plus was that tours of duty to Lebanon brought the Irish soldier into contact with facets of other cultures he might not otherwise have encountered. Fijibatt Medal parade in Qana attracted a large crowd. The band wore red jackets and white sarong—the foot drill display was excellently executed, the old Fijian way of life depicted in a specially constructed mini-village, the kava-kava passed round ...the root drink that contains a mild narcotic sedative.

The increasing Hezbollah activity brought for us many pre-dawn runs to the bunker. Normaintcoy's tinny alarm scratching at the air warned the section to get into shelter, Ops told us too via the 77 radio set. *Groundhog!* The noise would begin like distant thunder. Exploding rockets, rapid machine-gun fire, getting louder and louder, nearer. The SLA responding by firing tank rounds ... often we heard the buzzing of the Israeli pilotless drone as it toured the skies, photographing the terrain.

We slept with our Steyr rifles within hand's reach. The Steyr is an Austrian manufactured assault rifle with hair cross sights and is comprised of a hard plastic main body. Rumour had it that the Government exchanged a butter mountain or two for the weapons – subsequently it was called The Butter Gun, but this could have been down to the fact that soldiers suspected the rifle would melt if put too close to a fire. I mean, it was plastic.

The bunker itself contained rations and fresh water and medical supplies, a radio and field phone. Secure against ricochet and shell fragmentation, it would not have withstood a direct hit – you were aware of this when sitting there listening to the melee going on around you. But I pushed this to the back of my mind.

Once darkness fell, after such bombardments, we locked the main gate and the doors to the house. From the duty room upstairs the orderly NCO maintained a listening watch on the field phone and radio, and could see the gate—our electricity was derived from a pair of generators that droned 24 hours a day, each resting for 12 hours. One cranked up before the other was turned off. A sign affixed to the façade of the building read, 'Steadfast and Vigilant,' which wasn't the case when a 46 radio set was stolen from one of the patrol jeeps on a previous tour. You were aware that if things weren't done right that someone would see this and take advantage; steal ammo, even a weapon. In Lebanon, laxity presented opportunity.

***

Diary entry: Attacks on the SLA compounds by the Hezbollah grow brazen. Arriving into the section after having lunch in Camp Shamrock, there is a thunderous explosion. We park and hurry upstairs to the roof. On a dirt road across the wadi, a car is ablaze and gunfire is peppering it. In a copse of pine, fire is being directed at the compound from a heavy machine gun mounted on the bed of a jeep. Ricochets zing off the facade of the post, whistling past, causing us to take cover. Later we see Israeli gunships in action over the woods, but by then the Hezbollah has long gone to ground.

The Hezbollah aren't the guerrilla fighters of old who used to attack under the cover of darkness, ignoring the fact that the enemy had night-sights—on a few occasions poorly-trained armed elements when detected would hide behind boulders. This cover would be slowly obliterated by SLA heavy machine gun fire and the men shot dead. Now the Israelis and SLA are encountering a slick and professional outfit. Their roadside bombs and sniper attacks are making serious inroads into Israeli and SLA morale. In one incident an Israeli foot patrol was engaged in a fire-fight and gave chase to the armed elements, firing at them as they pursued. When they ran out of ammo the AE's turned and attacked.

Daring raids … The intensity of these engagements was such that I believed it was only a matter of time before something serious occurred that involved Irishbatt personnel – there was simply too much heat going around for one of us not to get badly burned, too many red flares from our positions indicating that the combatants were firing close to a UN position. Close to the end of the trip too, when fellas were rounding up the last of their presents, finding out what chalk they were on—it happened.

CHAPTER 8

A Norwegian MP from MP Coy arrived in Gallows Green around lunch-time. He said he'd carried out a drug search with a sniffer dog in a billet, found a quantity of cannabis in a locker, and had arrested the soldier to whom it belonged. He showed me the nugget; a scrap of Lebanese gold contained in a small blue Nivea tub. Enough for personal use. I recorded a statement under caution from the soldier and he ended up being awarded detention by the Battalion CO, which he served in Gallows Green. This incident highlighted the fact that drugs were being used in the area of operations by troops, even on checkpoint duty. I didn't think this was an isolated incident of cannabis use, nor did I think that it presented as major a problem as did the abuse of alcohol. I thought this because the misuse of drugs within the army wasn't prevalent—but the abuse of alcohol was—and created problems for the individual and the MP when an investigation was in progress. Interestingly, the army has of late introduced stringent and punitive penalties for anyone during a random selection process whose results show up as positive regarding drug usage. Perhaps, the same zero tolerance should also be applied to those who abuse alcohol?

A few times when investigating incidents of theft, soldiers I interviewed said they'd been drunk and couldn't remember any details that might progress the investigation. I had no doubt that they were telling the truth. It left me in a quandary—they'd admitted to breaking military law (it's an offence to be drunk) and so by right I should have cautioned them. Military Police used the same caution employed by civil police, and submitted a charge, AF (Army Form) 117.

A lot of the time—and this happened throughout all my tours of duty—friends and acquaintances volunteered information about certain people, certain activities. They were keeping me in the know. Nothing more. That was the height of their involvement and they'd made me aware of that. Intelligence had been provided and it was down to the Military Police to net the proof. On the other hand those engaged in illegal activity also had their own intelligence concerning the Military Police. The individuals who told me might have been merely passing information to draw a reaction; nudge me into saying or doing something rash —making untrue and unfounded allegations. People like to talk and UNIFIL thrived on ball-hops, things said that had absolutely no basis in truth, put out as a bit of craic by rumour mongers.

One day my friend told me there was a call for me from Ireland. This was late in the tour—28 September. In 16 days time the chalks home would commence and I would be on the first of them. The news related to Bernadette and the birth of our son, Barry. It's very hard to describe the emotion and depth of feelings that ran through me; relief, surprise and delight.

I made no diary entry that day.

I broke the news to the section and I could tell that some

thought I was mad to leave behind such a domestic situation. I had a beer to celebrate the arrival of my new son, but didn't enjoy it. I had this bad feeling in the pit of my stomach and a knot there that wouldn't unravel. That night, major attacks on the compounds occurred and we were in the bunker, listening to the radio traffic on the 77 set as fighting raged round us. Patsy was in the main house, frying sausages, while Mickey Rall and Paddy Barrett were on the rooftop watching the action unfold through field glasses.

News dripped through—an Irish soldier had been killed ...

Corporal Peter Ward from 'C' Company in Bra-Shit. He was the 35th Irish soldier to be killed while serving with UNIFIL. RIP.

Brendan Markey was detailed to travel with the remains by helicopter to Naqoura. He was the liaison officer, responsible for seeing the repatriation of the remains to Ireland. SIS, Special Investigation Section, MP Coy arrived up a day later and we assisted them with the investigation.

The circumstances leading to the fatal shooting were tough to hear. The fighting in the A.O. had been significant and unlike other mornings lasted well into daylight hours. In the dead of night a Mercedes car arrived at Al-Jurn checkpoint, coming from the Bra-Shit direction, in the general area where the Hezbollah were waging their campaign against what they called the, 'Occupying forces.' Al-Jurn or Post 5-10 was situated at a Y-junction. There was a gun tower and in it a sentry armed with a GPMG (General Purpose Machine Gun). Booms were in place across both sides of the Tibnin—Bra-Shit Road. Across from the Mag post there were civilian houses and shops, to the left of the post on the

Tulin Road to 'A' Company was a school, with a boundary wall overlooking the road.

Someone at the post looked in the rear seat of the car and saw a partially covered body. They refused entry to the driver. A stand-off ensued, with locals trying to diffuse the situation. When the driver made a call on his Motorola, the locals disappeared. Within minutes a convoy of civilian vehicles arrived at the scene. The occupants alighted and took up positions around the post. The Mag post was fired upon and in the hail of bullets the young soldier inside was seriously wounded in the stomach. Another Irish soldier was shown a grenade by an armed element who had taken up position behind the school wall. He was told to put his weapon on the ground. A rocket propelled grenade was then fired into the air. An Irish checkpoint some 400 metres away had a clear view of the incident and loosened four rounds at the wall of a house as a deterrent. This position came under fire from heavily armed elements who had outflanked it and taken up cover in a house occupied by a family.

Into this scene arrived an APC from 'C' company—Corporal Peter Ward was in the lead turret, exposed from the waist up. The APC was hit by a fusillade of rounds, one of which fatally wounded the corporal. Acting under instructions from 'C' Company HQ the APC returned to Bra-Shit.

When Corporal Ward had been hit, a young medic in the cab tried to render what medical aid he could in the circumstances to his stricken comrade, and felt bullets glancing off the bullet proof glass behind his head. AEs expended over 2,000 rounds in this sustained attack on a vulnerable UNIFIL position.

Video tapes of the night-time fighting, with the blood draped

APC, ended up for sale in Mingi shops a few days later but were withdrawn from the shelves by the traders after I suggested to Brendan that it wasn't right—in fact it stank. Travelling mingi men sold T-shirts that read, 'Hezbollah 1 – Ireland 0.'

Irishbatt was trying to control a situation that they never had control of to begin with. The situation in the AO at that time was extremely hostile; Hezbollah unlike the Amal was not benign in their regard towards UNIFIL. At the end of the day we too were foreign troops on their soil, loosely tolerated because of the humanitarian aid proffered by the battalions – Irishbatt down the years were always to the forefront when it came to providing resources to the local orphanage and villagers.

An incident such as this was always on the cards … the devil picked Al-Jurn.

I was dismayed by Hassan the interpreter when he tried to make excuses for Hezbollah's activities and didn't condemn the killing outright. It was sad 'but yeah, but no' sort of crap—stuff spewed from people trying to justify the taking of life.

Recording witness statements from individuals was particularly harrowing for all concerned. On occasion, interviews had to be halted to allow the soldier compose himself … and I wondered if it was proper to be recording statements from soldiers who were still so very obviously in shock and who perhaps needed counselling at the time and not a Military Policeman sitting in front of them. I didn't like doing it but I was under orders to take the statements—the trip was close to being over and the report had to be completed.

Two weeks later I was sitting in the back of truck in a convoy winding its way down the mountain, en route to Ben Gurion airport – Chalk 1. There were two of us; Little Spud was quiet, said he'd never, not if he lived to be a hundred years old, set foot in Lebanon again.

The skies were brightening and we fell to silence.

I was saying the same thing; I wouldn't be back.

On the flight home a news report of Corporal Ward's killing and a photograph of him in service uniform came on the in-flight TV screen. I couldn't hear what was being said because some people were talking, not paying any heed to the news. I thought 'Comradeship, my arse.' I felt there should have been a quiet moment of respect paid to the soldier. After all, we were going home without someone who should have been on the plane with us.

★★★

Barry was in his pram, sleeping, when I walked into the kitchen. He had a shock of black hair and his head carried a bruise from the birthing. Bernadette was well, looked radiant, proud—and Colin too … I remember the heat in the kitchen, the warm welcome … I was glad to be home.

At four in the morning I sat Barry on my knee in the kitchen and nursed him, feeding him. In the quiet, in the dim light, turf collapsing in the range, tears flowed …relief, regret—someplace else, a dad didn't make it. And I thought of his family and what they were going through as they watched the date of each chalk pass by.

CHAPTER 9

As glad as I was to be home, I couldn't help but feel constricted by the confines of the Irish barracks, and with a chance to earn some extra money for my growing family, I found myself, over the next couple of years, looking abroad again.

After a while I was a seasoned overseas campaigner. Along with my previous two-trips to Lebanon, I had done a tour of duty to Iraq as a military observer during the ceasefire in the Iran-Iraq war, a war that ran for eight years, resulting in over one million deaths. World War I tactics had been used there, and everywhere I looked I could see the craziness of that particular era; miles of deep trenches that dwarfed our landcruisers as they sloshed through the mud, passing torn ammunition boxes, split helmets and frayed webbing. Chemical weapons and mustard gas dropped from planes and helicopters killed many thousands of civilians.

In one village alone some 5,000 souls perished—an act as heinous and barbaric as that of 9/11, only not broadcast to the world. Halabjia was the name of the town, now empty, ghostly, no noise apart from the whine of our engines; a door beating against its frame and the wind's soulful lament. The official stance taken by the Iraqis was to deny that chemical weapons had been used. Facts are contrary: the Iraqis during their Anfal Campaign of 1988 set about levelling every Kurdish village within a 25 km radius of the border with Iran. This border is long and porous. The Iraqis did this to punish Kurdish elements who were assisting the Iranian army. In the Iran- Iraq war both nations won, lost, regained, and surrendered territories. The results of the Anfal campaign were harrowing to witness. We patrolled mountain regions, passing flattened villages, the wells filled in, dogs running wild, scenes from some doomsday movie.

I learned that Mustard gas burns the throat and mouth, and leaves a yellowy scum around the lips; an early indication of the type of gas used, revealed by close-up satellite pictures of the bodies lying on the streets. Iraq had been a different proposition to Lebanon—the people not as friendly, suspicious of the UN, endured shortages of essential food supplies and a hefty war tax on what foodstuffs were available. In addition they feared the Iranians and their own authorities, and this cast an almost surreal depression that hung in the atmosphere like an invisible pall. During my time in Iraq, I had learned of the death of Mannix Armstrong, who along with two other Irishbatt soldiers in south Lebanon, had driven over an anti-tank mine on a dirt road. Mannix had been a member of my MP probationers' course in 1981 but only stayed a few weeks. I think most soldiers, if asked, would list land mines as their greatest fear.

They are the silent enemy, lurking in the ground for 50 years and longer after a war has ended, a reminder that a war never really ends – it hibernates. Land mines are designed to mutilate, maim and kill – anti-personnel mines shred feet, legs and genitals and the screams of the victim strikes fear and panic into the soldier's colleagues – in an instant a mine has taken a colleague out of action and others too who now have to find the resources to help a comrade, and quickly. An anti-tank mine has two pressures: one primes under the roll of one wheel and the second wheel detonates.

Often in Lebanon and Israel, you'd see the landmines above ground and warning signs at the edges of the minefields—heavy rain moves the mines on to roads—territory gained, lost and then re-gained, minefield maps lost, those who sowed them dead or gone from the area. For an object that costs so little to manufacture; US$3, the destruction and human misery they harvest is unquantifiable. Much of the terrain in Northern Iraq was similar to the hilly terrain of Lebanon. And the blackness of the night in Sulaymaniyah was the same as the blackness of the night in Tibnin, and of course Kilbride.

Iraq was a mission that came up unexpectedly and people had to respond quickly. There wasn't much thought given to travelling, to be frank. I asked Bernadette, she said yes, and I put my name forward. I had the bug for travelling … and Iraq, well, it was exotic. And the pay was very good.

***

But Lebanon. I don't really know how it came up on the radar so suddenly. There was a shortage of volunteers, and I wasn't expecting my application to be successful. I spoke with Bernadette and as usual she agreed to my going. We were thinking of adding a small extension to the house and this tour would help fund its construction.

The form-up this time round took place in McDonagh Barracks, called after a signatory of the 1916 proclamation, a barracks no longer extant. McDonagh Barracks or GTD, General Training Depot, had been my original unit, where I had trained as a recruit and as a three-star private. I enjoyed my time there but disliked the frequent 24 hour guard duties, in particular Fire Piquet which required you to begin work at 0900am one day and finish the next at 1630 hrs. It was an anachronistic duty in an army kept so by successive governments through their lack of funding to buy proper equipment and transport. We'd wear a shirt and tie under our spick and span combat uniform to perform 24 hour guard duty in run-down barracks. Picture a butler in his finery mucking out a pig sty.

What all this has to do with a book about Lebanon is this— work conditions, the tedium of duty and routine barrack life fuelled a soldier's desire to take a break from such soul-blackening activities. Perhaps I would not have gone abroad as frequently as I had done if the pay and working conditions in my home environment had been up to scratch. In hindsight part of the problem lay in the fact that I was looking for excuses to travel abroad. I was finding it difficult to settle down. Minor things about home service irritated me. For instance, in Lebanon I armed and disarmed my own weapon, in Ireland I couldn't do that unless instructed to by an officer. This was a safety issue and I never read anything else into it—how could I? Accidental discharges of weapons happen, guys end up being wounded or killed, and there are near misses too. And this in a controlled weapon milieu.

Irish soldiers actually volunteered to serve abroad at this time. They wanted to go—a status which has now changed for the modern soldier who can be detailed to serve abroad. Lebanon was a break from the tedium of barrack life, an opportunity to earn extra money, to enjoy fine weather; it was a place where a soldier really soldiered.

***

19 April: *Diary entry*: The leaving doesn't get any easier. Goodbye is a horrible word. It hurts to look at the boys and know that – what? I'm stealing time from them—Is that mush?—Why am I thinking like this, now? My absence is improving their living circumstances – but why has this new notion crept into my mind? I don't mention my new feelings to Bernadette. Life is about trade-offs and hopes, right? No one gets everything they want, no-one's hopes have all come about. Right? Trade-off – time for money. It's an old equation. Loose scribbles here of American fighter planes shooting down two of their own choppers, killing 26 people. In Iran, television satellite dishes are banned.

Travelling overseas to Naqoura with me that summer were Pat Searle and Fran Hayden who were the company sergeants, corporals Peter Murphy, Liam Slattery, Gerry O'Rourke, and Greg Heffernan (whose brother Martin, I had served with in Iraq). I was acting sergeant, as were Ollie Griffin and Brendan Wrenne. The officers were Comdt Tom Creaton and a pay officer, Paul Kennedy. Billy O'Shea was the Company Sergeant Major.

Tom Creaton was relaxed and respectful of all ranks and his work ethic, like Brendan Markey's; thoughtful, methodical and imaginative. Pat Searle would serve his first three months as Dogface Tyre, and be successful in smashing a major smuggling racket. Fran Hayden was a gilty soldier, that is one who kept himself and his uniform ultra-smart, leading by example. He was employed as collator and Crime Reader in an office with a highly efficient Lebanese secretary called Aida who had worked with MP Coy since 1978. Fran was meticulous in his work and always sought to improve upon the previous incumbent's legacy —this job required a special eye for detail and sometimes long hours and could be exasperating if the final reports handed in by the relevant in- company sections for reviewing arrived without important witness statements, technical or medical reports.

***

I liked Lebanon, travelling, and again the money aspect, too. The first trip was about earning money, the medal, and wanting the experience. The others were done because the opportunity was there to earn even more extra money. Soldiers weren't paid a lot in those days—they seemed to be made suffer for their safe tenure of employment, and so the chance to earn roughly £4,000 wasn't something easily spurned. I was also in a corps that had a national complement of about 500 personnel and some of these would have been ineligible for overseas services because of age restrictions. On top of this, the recruitment stop-start policy had resulted in only a trickle of new Military Policemen coming into the corps and this was never enough to satisfy the increasing overseas demand. As a result of this, overseas opportunities were up for grabs.

The evening of my departure for the third time, I said goodbye to Bernadette and the boys. Colin was 10 and used to the goodbyes. He wanted a G- shock watch sent home, green, he said. Barry was 18 months; too young to fully realise what was going on around him. In time it would be he who grounded me from travelling abroad.

My parents dropped into McDonagh Barracks to say a quick goodbye. Mam said that Dad had a bad mouth ulcer. One that had gone down his throat. My brother Shane was getting married in the summer. Looking back on it, I was tough, stubborn and wayward, uncompromising because I wouldn't come home for the wedding. Not altogether the healthiest of mindsets, but I resented being pressurised and manipulated into doing things. It ran against my grain.

Not many people who knew me would have laid a tenner at 500 to 1 for me to serve 21 years in the army without being charged. I should have been, but some fine footwork off the ropes led me to safety; I have scars on my tongue from biting on it so often.

***

This time, I was employed in the Special Investigation Section. This section was responsible for the investigation of serious crime within UNIFIL and for carrying out random drug searches, rotation luggage searches et al. The officer-in-charge was Finnish — Kari, and the office usually comprised a rotating staff of six; because of leave, detachment, rotation home. The hardy annuals during that tour were Valimaki; Finnish; Alifoh; Ghanaian; Matt; Norwegian, Ollie Griffin; Irish; and myself.

Parade in the mornings was taken at 7am by the major, Billy, who now and then forgot himself and gave the order in Irish to come to attention, confusing the other nationalities. After this we went to our respective offices to begin the day's work. Kari was a Finnish civilian police officer and like a lot of Finns he was into body building. The Finns had their own sauna in MP Coy and we envied them this as much as we envied the sniffer dogs in their air-conditioned kennels. Kari asked each of us for updates on our case loads, issuing new investigations as they came on stream. The day's tasks were discussed as well as special duties allotted for the coming days.

I shared a room with Fran Hayden in prefab accommodation. The prefab terrace was called, 'Patrick Street'. Mosquito coils burned the night long, leaving a pile of fine ash in the mornings. A tall fan stood centre-floor, whirled, turned in a 180 degree angle, taking the sting out of the mugginess.

On our first days there we left our uniforms for tailoring into a tailor on Mingi Street. The shirts needed tightening, a seam sown in the slacks and elastic put in the leg ends so they'd fit snugly round the boots. Fran wasn't satisfied with the workmanship and left his clothes in on three occasions. Finally he collected them and was content that his gear was the finished article. That evening when I was lying on my bunk breathing in mosquito coil fumes, reading, Fran ironed his shirt and trousers, putting in a crease across the shoulders with a starch spray he had bought specially. He put the brassards on his shirt, and his name badge, and hung them outside his locker. Grabbing his toilet bag he padded off in his flip-flops to the shower room. In his absence I exchanged his perfectly tailored shirt for my inferior one.

The next morning after showering he put on his shirt and said, 'Jesus, I'm still not 100 per cent happy with that woman's tailoring. You're right, I think she is going blind.'

'Maybe, but mine is all right.'

'You'd wear anything.'

'I would.'

I asked Ollie and Brendan to call in to Fran at intervals and to casually remark upon the shabbiness of his shirt, and advise him to have it done like Murt's, which fitted him perfectly.

Fran didn't cop it till much later.

Writing of tailors, in 1992 I'd gone to a tailor in Tibnin to have clothes altered—army uniforms, you can't wear them as issued as they look crappy—and when he put the stump of his arm against my hip to hold the tape in check I thought I was going to throw up on the shine of his crown. He was a one- armed tailor.

★★★

Break-ins and theft of property from UNIFIL stores was endemic throughout that tour of duty. Propane gas bottles, electric cable, generators, petrol and oil, food stuffs, were some of the things stolen in much quantity. And I was tasked with investigating many of these cases.

I was called upon one morning to investigate the reported theft of an electrical cable from a UNIFIL store close to a French position on the coastal road to the border. Almost opposite the stores was a half-finished hotel owned and managed by the Nagm sisters, who were originally from Beirut.

The store was an enclosed compound with a high wall. In a frayed and tattered Rubb tent stood large wooden spools holding black electric cable.

The thieves fed the cable out through a hole in the bottom of the wall, an onerous task that must have taken much time. At the back of the wall was a space large enough to park a pick-up, this hidden from view by a derelict building, formerly a brothel.

I took my photographs, drew the sketch, and during the course of this, while I was outside the stores, Rose Nagm approached me. She was about 60, henna-coloured hair, a little wary of me.

She said, 'They take my cable.'

'Your cable?'

'Yes, yes, my cable. They take into the camp.'

She called a man from the hotel. He was an electrician.

Rose said, 'He is working for me, and I need the cable. The French take it this morning.'

I said I'd check it out and got into the Land Cruiser and entered the HQ, pulling in front of the French guard room. A soldier showed me the cable, a sizeable length. I rang a Field Service electrician who came down and said the cable wasn't UNIFIL property. Rose was grateful to see the return of her cable and I lived on free pizza for the rest of the trip. Rose and her sister were fluent French speakers and preferred to speak it, but their English was good enough to provide me with scraps of information. The ringleader behind the theft of UNIFIL stores was a man from the village of Beit-Leif—Bay Lif—to whom we gave the sobriquet; *The Thief from Beit-Leif.* Rose also told me about the time they saved a Polish soldier from drowning. It was during a time of curfew and he had tried to swim from his quarters, round the back of the hotel, to the brothel which obviously unbeknownst to him had been shut down that day, across the road. They laughed at the memory.

In the hotel I was introduced to a man by the name of Kassis, who was a high-ranking officer in the SLA. He didn't say much but said he would liaise with the OGL, Observer Group Lebanon, as he knew some of the officers. The OGL, by virtue of their role, could go places and speak with people no MP had access to; OGL officers worked in small teams and were located at special 'watch' occasions, and had built up a sound intelligence network. Observer Group Lebanon had been active in Lebanon since 1958, some 20 years before UNIFIL began operations in south Lebanon. They were, I suppose, a variety of troubleshooter, and their job was not without its dangers. In the present conflict—2006—four OGL died when an Israeli shell hit their position.

Personally, I liked to spend as little time as possible in the office. Along with Kari's briefing there was also a 10am briefing from the MP Ops officer and once a week the dogfaces from the different detachments arrived in to give a stat and situation report—with the noise of Italair heading out to sea, shaking the office and the sweltering heat, if you could busy yourself elsewhere, you did so.

Some time into the tour a teacher said he had important information and wanted to speak to the MPs and OGL. We met in a room off a camera shop on Mingi Street. He was a tall well-dressed man, nervous. His spiel went something like this …

'I know about the robberies—it is terrible—the UN do much good work here for the people and I am disgusted with how the

UN is being treated. I have information about the man who does all this damage —and I want nothing for myself, you see—I want to do only the proper thing …'

Someone, I think an OGL officer, said, 'That's very good …'

'But you see I am a teacher and do not get paid very much – what I tell you is very dangerous for me. I need $2,000.'

He looked at us and we looked at him. I shook my head, got up and walked out, leaving the OGL officers behind. To tell you the truth I was pissed off and very much down in myself and in no mood to be dealing with an asshole. I had other things on my mind. An hour before the meeting I'd received word that my dad had been diagnosed with throat cancer and was facing into a life-saving operation.

11 June: *Diary entry*: News of dad's illness—you don't expect to hear stuff like this. That's stuff for other people to hear. I feel lousy …I'm thinking of things I hadn't thought of for a long time. Memories. Think of Dad, too, about when the news caught him, his reaction, feel for him. And Mam. I don't want to write about it, nor think about it. But there's no getting away from thinking …

CHAPTER 10

One thing I've learned from being in the army; Quartermasters are important people if you want to make life as comfortable as possible for yourself. They know it too, and are wise to anyone sucking up to them, in much the same way as a Lotto millionaire is wary of strangers who want to get too close to him and his new fortune. A QM is sometimes called Q, and the word Q is known in some quarters as the Source; God. Q has the magic signature to release for you a new mosquito net, a fan that doesn't creak as it dances all night long, kerosene for your heater, a heater … Q decides whether or not you pay to replace a piece of lost equipment. If he wants, he can write it off as training loss, or due to wear and tear. I had become friendly with the MP Quartermaster, QM Epeli Konasau, over coffee in the MP Club, and it was a naturally-struck friendship.

Back in Fiji, Epeli was a kava farmer; a tall well-built, easy-going man with an infectious laugh. He was about 45 and had grey in the curls of his hair. He had a slow and easy gait that I never saw quicken. Fijians served for a year abroad. The logistics of travelling from and to the South Seas islands every half-year simply involved too much organisation and was a costly exercise.

At that time the Fijians were also committed to providing troops to the Sinai. The Irish used to have a commitment to Sinai, too, but were withdrawn in the aftermath of the Dublin-Monaghan bombings in the seventies—the uncertainty of the times—the Government believed the battalion might be needed at home. Overseas service afforded me the opportunity to see how other armies operated and I realised that in the heel of the hunt, armies are the same the world over. The situation—SNAFU—Situation Normal All Fucked Up, doesn't just apply to the Irish army.

The tour of duty in 1994 threw up solid friendships in the shape of Epeli, Ollie Griffin and Alifoh, a Ghanaian Warrant Officer. I think of all my tours abroad, it was the one trip where I had most need of friends. To meet three whom I could open up to and they to me, well it was a rare happening to find three within a six-month period. I was lucky.

But I learned a lot about peoples' sensitivities. One incident comes to mind. The SIS Section kept a figurine of a fat monk atop a filing cabinet and when its habit was raised its penis swung up. Someone decided to write Alifoh's name across the monk's arse. When the habit was raised he laughed but lost the head when the figurine was turned and he saw his name across the white butt. The crimson showed through the dark of his cheeks and he stormed from the office, the slam of the door shaking the prefab and sending reams of paper on flights to the floor. None of us knew what to make of it. Alifoh was always in good humour, gregarious and primed for a laugh, so we didn't think this bit of horseplay would rattle him. I'd to call down to Alifoh's billet the next day after he failed to appear on parade or report in for work. He opened the door, swell of his belly pushing against his white singlet, a bowl of uneaten foo foo (made from yam) on the table just inside the door.

'It was no good joke,' he said. 'Not funny. Not nice.'

I stepped inside and said, 'Yes, you're right. Look, come back to work. We covered for you this morning with the CSM ... but we can't keep doing it. Come on, knock the problem in its tracks, yeah?'

He lifted his eyebrows and shrugged, said, 'Okay, after the tea-break, after the Ops brief ... I hate the ops brief.'

'Good.'

That was one monk who never got to air his dick again. The incident served to remind me that every soldier, no matter his nationality, had lows while serving in Lebanon and owned sensitive personal issues. No soldier left his problems at home; he brought them with him.

My father's illness continued to play on my mind. Mam didn't want me to come home. She said Dad would lose heart and think the worst if he saw me coming through the hospital doors. I felt as though I had boxed myself in by saying I wasn't travelling home for my brother's wedding.

Dad had gotten the cancer in a part of the body where it was treatable and therefore had a high chance of cure. If the cancer had occurred in his stomach he would not have survived. If it had happened to him five years earlier he wouldn't have had much of a chance either —medical science is progressing all the time.

He got over his operation thanks to the skilled staff at St. James Hospital, but I was quite aware throughout my trip that the father who had said goodbye to me in McDonagh Barracks would not be the same man on my return.

Dad is an easy going sort of man. He likes his pint. He had quit smoking years ago, long before his illness struck. In his younger days he was a jump jockey and rode winners for Charlie Weld, including the Power Gold Cup and the Jameson Gold Cup on a horse called Coniston. He worked with horses all his life and was foreman to the powerful Dermot Weld stable on the Curragh until he fell ill. He was 59 years old when touched by cancer's black hand. But I had time now to digest the news of Dad's illness and saw that he had a good chance of surviving. I immersed myself in work, my writing, keeping a diary. I kept my mind occupied insofar as it was possible.

***

I used to write short stories when I was in my early teens—I had it in my head to write detective yarns. I didn't write throughout my 20s and began to write in my early 30s, lured to it again for some obscure reason that escapes definition. I had made up my mind to retire from playing soccer and was looking about for another interest, something to pass the time, something that I might enjoy. I began by writing short stories and articles, fostering a sole ambition to pen a collection of short stories, a form of writing I've had pretty decent success with. The collection, however, eluded me.

Regularly I walked and jogged the 6 kilometres to and from the border. At night I thought of Dad and what he was going through, the suffering, the worry about tests to see if the cancer had been contained, the skin grafts he had to undergo as the surgeons needed to re-shape his jaw line, the distortion of his voice. Many people don't get to think about not hearing their father's voice again until he has gone from their lives ... at least we still had him. Thinking on the situation from a remove of 12 years, the mental and emotional strength I drew on were traits Dad possessed too, for if the fight wasn't in him to live he wouldn't have pulled through his ordeal. His operation was a life saving one—he had a fighting chance of survival —the consultant could have shaken his head and told him he hadn't even got that much.

I always prayed. This habit wasn't imbued in me from childhood, in fact it was the opposite as I rebelled against being forced to learn prayers off by heart. The nuns, for the most part wicked creatures who taught me, said I wasn't ready to make my first communion. This bothered people but not me, and not until they brought me in to the convent for Saturday morning tuition did I learn my prayers. Honest to Christ, when I think about it ... a joke scenario really; beating the love of Christ into a child's hand. Some nuns and teachers were terrorists in the classroom. In my schooldays a key element of a teacher's training prowess was the ability to instil fear, not respect, into pupils. Fear doesn't work forever though. People get fed up being afraid and eventually they react in some shape or form. When I got older I bought a Bible and began to read it every day. Still do. I wanted to find out what was being spoken about at Mass, to think things out for myself. I suppose you could say the opportunity to visit the Holy Land was also a factor in my decision to travel abroad, albeit not a major one. In 1985 I'd travelled to the Holy Land with Mossy and John Hamill, visiting Jerusalem and Bethlehem, and sensed this special energy when in the cave under the altar in the Church of the Nativity. Perhaps the fuse was lit in my subconscious by the memories of Christmases past. In any regard, it was special. I think everyone sometimes gets that feeling and says to himself, 'Yeah, this it right, this feels so right,' without ever being able to finger the pulse of why exactly it is.

I was writing a lot of short stories, selling them to the likes of *Ireland's Own, Ireland's Eye,* and *Woman's Way.* Margaret Galvin was the editor of *Ireland's Own* and she gave me great encouragement. My work, writing, prayer, focused me. I never doubted that Dad wouldn't make it, but there were times I sank really low when I thought about the pain he was suffering.

Billy O'Shea sent me as Dogface to Metulla in northern Israel for five weeks. I drove there with William, a Ghanaian, and of course, got lost on the way up, driving along a winding uphill route through probably the only forest in Israel. We found our way eventually, stopping in Kiryat Shemona for a coffee and a sandwich. The name is Hebrew for *Town of the Eight,* after eight Jewish settlers killed at nearby Tel Hai in 1920. The town's proximity to the Lebanese border made it a favourite target for rocket attacks by Palestinians, and later Amal and Hezbollah. Rockets rained on the town by Hezbollah, probably initiating the Israeli bombardment of Qana, Fijibatt HQ, during which 106 civilians lost their lives.

Metulla itself was established in 1896 with a grant from the Rothschild family.

It is a town of fine gardens and like most towns in Israel is spotlessly clean. Metulla is an Arabic name and means *Overlooking.* It is situated right on the border with Lebanon, and UNIFIL troops from Norbatt and Finbatt passed through its border crossing on a daily basis, on leave or during rotation. Hence the need for UNIFIL Military Police. Metulla lives up to its name, as it does indeed overlook barbed wire, the security fence, concrete fortifications and the Iyon valley on the other side.

Like Nahariya, we were quartered in a house on the first floor in Dudevan Street. Seru, a Fijian, opened the front door to us. He had two burnt chickens on the kitchen table, said he'd hoped to have dinner ready for us, but had fallen asleep. There was a smell of burned potatoes, too. The place was like the inside of a sweaty sock. I looked round and said, 'Let's clean up...' The border didn't open on Sundays, so we worked a rota of 6am to Noon and Noon to 6pm between us, with the third day off. Not exactly an exacting work schedule. It was actually quite easy-going, but as Dogface I was responsible for the day to day running of the detachment, from compiling reports to buying in propane gas from Kiryat Shemona, to ensuring that our two patrol vehicles were serviced at the designated mileage recorded in their vehicle log books. Every UNIFIL vehicle had a log book with its registration number on its Hessian-like cover—they were pocket insets to hold the necessary documentation; mileage out, mileage in —a Paz station petrol book for filling up in Israel. Peacekeepers didn't pay for fuel. We tanked up at the station and they forwarded the docket on to UNIFIL HQ. One half of the invoice and other paperwork was handed in to Playtime, the MP Transport NCO, at the weekly Dogface meeting. In Lebanon, we filled up at UNIFIL controlled pumps. If we wanted a UNIFIL vehicle for touring in Israel we booked it a fortnight in advance.

All in all, Metulla was a nice enough place to be; certainly not the worst. I was able to use the facilities at the Canada House

Leisure Centre and had my first real massage, given by a Russian woman with hands like concrete and fingers like the tines of a garden fork. When she was finished she slapped me across the arse and then again, probably mistaking my shocked silence for a 'please do it again'.

'You get Jacuzzi and sauna for half-hour and then you come back to me ... okay for you?'

'Sure.'

I got my red arse out of there. I did have to try to keep the other guys in some sort of order, for professional and personal reasons. We had to share the same living space, and work together, so it was important to get along, but with different languages and different cultures, sometimes this wasn't easy, especially with people coming and going all the time. Seru returned to MP Coy, and his replacement was a Polish MP called David, and he had little English when it suited him.

11 July: *Diary entry:* I arrive back in the detachment one evening to find William close to tears in the sitting room. William is inoffensive and sensitive. He has served in Liberia and seen action there—says it is the worse place in the world. And that the Liberian ladies used to sell themselves for food. He wears a Saint Anthony medal around his neck, says that near where he lives in Ghana all the churches had been swept away in a flood, except for Saint Anthony's. I ask him what's wrong, thinking he might have heard bad news from home.

He gives a slight wave of his hand and says, 'Nothing ...' I persist and he nods. He doesn't look me in the eye, remaining focused on the fuzzy TV. I go into the kitchen and put the kettle on, check to see what bread there is, when I hear David's voice in the sitting room. Mouthing off at William, his tone derogatory.

'Give me the keys,' he says harshly, his voice slurred. David isn't aware of my presence.

'For what?' I say, from behind where he is standing.

He faces me, unsteady on his feet, 'I want to go to Kiryat Shemona.'

'I'll bring you,' I say evenly.

'I can drive.'

'No, no, you get your gear together and we'll go, now.'

'Gear?' His eyebrow travels high, puzzled.

'Your clothes, your equipment—I'm bringing you to Naqoura.'

He pales, smooths his gelled hair.

'I told you when you came here; no drink in the detachment.'

He doesn't say a word.

'Why were you giving William a hard time?'

He shrugs and starts to speak gibberish, his tone that he'd used toward William. I lift my voice and it is like I've slapped him. He is of a higher rank than a sergeant and in his mind I am being insubordinate.

In that short and vital pause, escalation or de-escalation is decided upon. The fog in his head clears and he says, 'Sorry,' and then looks at William and repeats it. William offers no acknowledgement.

David asks me not to tell the CSM. Billy O'Shea would run through him like a dose of salts.

The next morning was a day off and I left David in the detachment. He had a sore and guilty looking head and he'd spoken to William in a mild tone, trying to entice him into a conversation, but William remained frosty.

The border was a five-minute drive away. There was a nest of souvenir and coffee shops in front of the border gates; a small path led to a rock that had two steel masts embedded in it, holding steel flags of Lebanon and Israel. This is called The Good Fence because a Lebanese woman had once brought her ailing baby to the wire and handed him over to an Israeli doctor, who a week later returned the child fit and well to his mother. The Good Fence is symbolic, I suppose, an example of one human helping another. I thought the steel flags symbolic of intransigence; set in stone and steel and leaning away from each other.

Usually at the border post I sat alone in a small office, reading, waiting for the Israeli Liaison officer to knock on the door and say we were in business. Naturally, the liaison officers had excellent English. Their unit flash was the motif of an antlered deer and they drove an old grey Willies jeep, a relic from World War II. The ablution areas were similar to those found in Coolmoney Camp, in the Glen of Imaal; primitive.

Soccer is a universal language and the liaison officers liked to talk about the World Cup and Ireland's chances—they'd been delighted to see the Irish turn over the Italians and were impressed by Riverdance. They liked to speak about anything other than the world at the doorstep, their never-ending war with their cousins. Unlike paranoid Iraqi officers they didn't bother to curtain their wall with maps of the war theatre, and now and then when in a conversation they'd ask me about a village in Lebanon, not to glean information from me about it, but to see if I knew the lie of the land. Within a couple of milliseconds I had the tip of my finger on the spot on the map, and sometimes I could tell them about the positions of old compounds, abandoned because they'd lost their strategic importance. Those MP Op briefings came in handy!

The MPs carried out the same duties as at Roshaniqra border crossing, but in Metulla the Israeli mechanics devoted more time to searching UN vehicles, and if the UN driver betrayed any signs of agitation or annoyance the search lasted longer. Military Police were present in case the searcher found something and to watch that they didn't plant anything. Personal searches of UN personnel were done by a hand-held scanner that blipped when passing over metal—UN soldiers had attempted to bring pistols into Israel, bringing them home to Finland or Norway. Lebanese civilians permitted to work in Israel also crossed the border. These workers were vital to the Israeli economy, in much the same way as the foreign workers in the Ireland of today. We had nothing to do with the searching of Lebanese civilians. Shortly after my return to MP Coy, an apparently innocuous video cassette exploded at Metulla border crossing, seriously wounding a person.

***

William wasn't a driver and he'd asked me a week before to bring him to Nazareth and Cana; places he hadn't visited. I'd been to Nazareth before with Ollie O'Flaherty in 1985. When William and I were in the Church of the Annunciation, I remembered Ollie. He was a great guy. I thought of the time we were coming back from Irishbatt and had driven up to the first boom at Charlie Swing-gate when the gunner in the Sherman tank fired a heavy machine gun over our heads. Ollie said quietly, 'Hand me my Gustav, Murt.'

'For what? To use against a fuckin' tank?'

'Open the boom.'

The atmosphere was poisonous. With knees gone to jelly I got out of the car, swung back the gate and allowed our jeep through. Ollie said they were bastards. I said they were bigger bastards than what he thought. That trip, the end of it, during our re-pat medical, Ollie emerged from the doctor's clinic, fuming,

'He said I'd be dead in ten-years if I didn't quit the smoking ... the nerve of him,' he said, grievously offended, exhaling smoke. That was Ollie.

Nazareth was built on a hill, and there isn't all that much to see of what is purported to be Mary's house, apart from a few antiquated steps that are railed off within the church. Impressive, though, are the icons and frescoes in Saint Gabriel's church and the ancient graffiti carved around the doorway. Mary's Well, also known as the Virgin's fountain, is located inside the church and some believe that the Archangel Gabriel appeared to Mary here and that the waters have the power of healing. It wasn't much in evidence considering what was going on in the background.

After my detachment in Metulla had ended, I went back into the Investigation Section, where as with everything else in Lebanon, the news was mixed, the situation lying somewhere between good and very bad. Ollie Griffin briefed me on the killing of two Fijian soldiers at a checkpoint on a coastal road. The Thief from Beit Leif was rumoured to have been caught and currently held in the notorious Khiam prison … probably true because the stores and warehouses had begun to enjoy a crime free spell.

CHAPTER 11

The Fijian soldiers had stood in sentry boxes at either end of a checkpoint outside the walls of their base in Al-Mansuri village. They wore blue UN helmets with *UN* stencilled in white, the *N*'s middle line not connecting with its partners. Chin-straps dog-eared, smelling of old leather and sweat. They had carried cheap camouflage wallets that held their UN I.D. card, a family photograph, a wooden crucifix; Christ absent.

In the minutes preceding the drive-by shootings, the village had assumed an unearthly silence. A Mercedes approached the checkpoint, accelerated, and travelling at speed, swept through the CP, its occupants firing upon and killing the Fijians instantly. The perpetrators were known to the UN and Lebanese authorities. It's important to keep in mind that at that time, Hezbollah, the guerrilla outfit, was a member of the Lebanese Parliament and in reality UNIFIL soldiers had been shot and killed by the very institution that had invited them into their country. MP Coy's final investigation report would recount the events of the day as they unfolded, include witness statements, post mortem reports and a photograph album. But as for apprehending the culprits, this was well nigh impossible.

Much of what informants told Military Police often went unrecorded, not even logged in the file's case notes. Police merely presented the facts, if they had other information but couldn't get a 'lock' on evidence, it wasn't submitted in a final report. It was said that the soldiers were killed in reprisal for a beating and a badly broken hand that Fijians had inflicted on a Lebanese civilian. The Fijians patrolled a dirt track called the McKenzie Road and some times they chanced upon armed elements about to launch rockets across the border, so naturally they prevented it from happening. Those who knew the full circumstances kept it to themselves, leaving the rest of us to merely hazard guesses at the real truth, the jigsaw incomplete. Often, Fijian soldiers, whenever we required them for interview, mysteriously went to ground, shifted from post to post, not alone in the case just mentioned but in some others, too. This circling of the wagons was organised by the Fijians in case it yielded another truth relating to another matter and to someone else.

30 July: *Diary entry*: Netanya is a seaside resort about 35 km from Tel Aviv, and its main street is lined with cafes and patisseries. It is named after Nathan Strauss, an American philanthropist, and is a major industrial centre specialising in diamonds, citrus packing and beer making. I travel alone in the minibus, driving past the blue Perspex covered footbridge leading into the shopping mall, a landmark I had been told to watch out for, followed by my counting junctions till I reach a roundabout where I turn left. Anyway, I get lost and pull over beside a phone kiosk and ring the detachment. Concentrating on driving is enough for my mind to do, it seems—directions,

no matter how simple, confuse me—information lost in the flow of my thoughts and other concerns.

'Hello, MP,' the voice says. The line goes dead. I ring again.

'Hello, MP.' Dead. He's hung up on me. I call MP Coy and get directions. When I knock on the detachment door I'm let in by a Nepalese MP, who is all smiles.

'Where is everyone?' I say, but he hasn't enough English to tell me.

'Coffee?' he says.

There are three others on detachment: a French MP called Toure, Epeli, and the Ghanaian, Opare. I read the unit journal. No entries that day; not even the morning situation report to MP Coy has been logged. The Nepalese MP shows me to my bedroom; a small box room to the back that has a skinny balcony off it. I make up my bed and put away my clothes. The apartment is spacious, if dated. The sitting room runs into a small study and a kitchen. There are four bedrooms and two bathrooms. A typewriter sits on the Formica topped table in the office. I'll write here most mornings. I'd bought a Casio electric typewriter and a plethora of cassette ribbons from Ali in Mingi Street, and am anxious to get used to it. Ali said they were the business. Naturally. Toure and Opare arrive. Shake of hands, introductions. Opare said they'd been on patrol to Tel Aviv, Epeli is in town at the market, it's his day off.

Netanya was busier than Metulla. Troops visited from UNDOF to take a break from keeping the thin blue line in the Golan Heights, keeping a distance between Israeli and Syrian forces.

Others came from UNIFIL. The owner of *The Scotsman*, Yitzik, was friendly towards the MPs and always gave us free coffee in return for our help whenever anything boisterous started to look like it might get out of hand. A presence was usually enough to stop any trick-acting.

Woody, the prostitute who plied her trade on the street, offered only blow jobs if you were married and every time she saw me she gave a blow in the ear job, telling me what hotels the UNIFIL soldiers were staying in, relaying this information without request, telling me so I would know where to go if any UNIFIL personnel got into trouble, as occasionally happened. She was a feisty character, much too old for the game she was involved in. She wore a red dress and moved like a fast flowing galleon through the main street, her eye out for a potential client. If you wanted to see examples of her at work, and she had a habit of showing these without warning, catching a person off-guard as he assumed, naturally perhaps, that she was about to show snaps of her family and that, she would be only too happy to oblige. No faces revealed. Just cocks of her walk.

★★★

A call rang in about 7am. An Israeli police woman said she had a Fijian UNIFIL soldier in a cell in Tel Aviv. She wanted us to collect him. He'd been arrested for being drunk and disorderly. I called Epeli and we drove to Tel Aviv. He wore these yellow-framed sunglasses, looked at me and said, 'Are they okay?'

'Yeah, but only in the car. I wouldn't wear them anywhere else.'

He laughed, said, 'No one will steal these.'

It turned out that he'd had several pairs of sunglasses stolen.

Traffic was light going into Tel Aviv and there was no problem with finding the location because Epeli knew the way, like someone who'd been there before many times. At Reception I spoke with a police officer who listened, pulled a face and made a call. He had ink stains on his blue collar and looked like he was having a hard day.

Jerking his thumb over his shoulder, he said, 'Follow the yellow line ...'

The Wizard of Oz ...

Lines of different coloured paint patterned the concrete floor. The yellow line brought us to basement cells. The soldier behind bars was small for a Fijian and had a truculent face, ready to create more trouble. When Epeli arrived in seconds later—the slow ambling gait —all notions of trouble abandoned his face. Like ice under a hot sun.

Epeli spoke earnestly to him. The soldier put his shirt on and came with us, without so much as a quibble on his lips.

In the minibus I asked what had happened and he said, 'I was minding my own business, drinking a few beers when these guys jumped me ...'

He had minor abrasions above his left eyebrow and a scratch to his cheekbone. Back at the detachment I rang MP Coy and briefed the Duty NCO, then I called MP Nahariya and arranged a meeting point at the usual place outside Haifa, at a filling station, where we'd hand over our prisoner to them for conveyance to the border where the MP patrol would bring him to a cell in MP Coy.

I noticed something about our guest and asked him to turn his wrist: he had a black Swastika tattoo.

'You know the meaning, the significance of that, don't you?' I said.

He shook his head. He had no idea what I was on about.

'That's a Nazi symbol.'

Blank eyes.

'They would have turned on you for that tattoo. The Nazis killed millions of Jews …'

I felt like a fool saying this.

But.

'Really?' those numb eyes said.

★★★

It was a sheer novelty waking every morning to sun and birdsong. Surreal almost, idyllic. Money in my pocket, cars at my disposal, a day off, mine to do whatever I liked, within reason. I walked a lot, visited museums and book shops, and during my walks twice on the same route the same day, I witnessed first hand the ferocity of Israeli women. One lost her temper in the post office and was screaming through the Perspex at a man who had just switched off and was no longer listening. Another woman in the street berated her husband, I presumed; a blazing row that was worrisome and looked at any moment as though it might spiral out of control. Any row I'd witnessed or been involved in before suddenly seemed pretty tame by comparison. Those women were capable of committing murder with their tongues. They certainly knew how to boil the air. And in this they proved themselves to be very much like Lebanese women of whom I'd once witnessed seven or eight surround a bridegroom and berate him with tongue and handbag. All the groom could do was ward off the blows and wait for their ire to be spent. These women had a lot of ire to spend.

When on foot patrols with my Nepalese colleague, he insisted on walking two steps behind me; this wasn't a tactical ploy but rather a show of respect. Nepalese drivers behind the wheel of a heavy truck, descending a winding mountain road, took a hand off the wheel to salute oncoming UN traffic; a practice frowned upon, and discouraged and attributable to at least one serious accident. I'd gesture him forward and he'd stay alongside me for a distance and then fall back.

***

A week before my return to MP Coy, I was tasked with travelling to Haifa, Rambam Hospital, to check on the condition of a Finnish soldier who Italair had flown in from Finbatt. Flights such as these were called, 'Medivacs'—medical evacuations. Whenever the Hueys were wound up to fly outside of their routine night-time exercises you knew they were off to the Hills to collect a soldier and bring him to the UN Hospital in Naqoura, and perhaps later after medical assessment of his injuries, onwards to Rambam Hospital.

Outside the operating theatre a surgeon handed me a garden knife. It had a wooden handle and a rusted blade. The soldier had been a patient in Finbatt Regimental Aid Post, RAP, suffering from a psychiatric disorder. The week before he had attempted to cut his throat. A loaded Sauer pistol was found under his pillow, a weapon he'd had in his possession for some time. It caused me to wonder about the fragility and workings of the mind; he'd stuck a garden knife in the side of his throat and yet had a pistol.

I put the knife in an evidence bag, labelled it, and would bring it with me when I crossed the border on Tuesday, my last day in Netanya.

Kari Huhta, OIC SIS, welcomed me back into the fold. It was the season of the Ghanaian rotation and SIS, the entire section, was driving to Kafr Dunin, Ghanbatt HQ, for a job involving the search of luggage and equipment. During a visit to Finbatt HQ in May, Kari had brought me into the officer's mess for lunch, despite my objections. A Ghanaian officer looked at my rank insignia and said, 'This facility is for officers.'

I was about to say, 'I know, I'm slumming it,' but with a look at Kari and seeing the embarrassment on his face—I saw that he was getting annoyed and about to say something—I said, 'It's okay, don't dig a hole for yourself.'

Segregation like this between professional soldiers is indicative of and mirrors a class society. This culture was alien to Huhta as he was a civilian police officer and not attuned to the nuances and anomalies of military life. Though he was learning—once when investigating a serious incident in Qana, a Fijian officer said he would talk only to Huhta and not the MP sergeant, which was me. So, I excused myself and went to the PX, bought a cola and sat and talked to some of the soldiers who told me all and more that their officer had to say. Driving home I asked Huhta what the officer had to say and he replied, 'Nothing much.'

I told him what nothing much was and he looked sidelong

at me and smiled. When we arrived, a female Ghanaian officer brought us into a room and invited us to sit down and drink some of the beers on the table. Her people would do the search, we were not to worry.

Relax. Drink. Please.

Huhta's lips parted, his eyes widened.

'We will search,' he said.

The things I heard about searches: a Ghanaian officer had dissembled a jeep and crated it as cargo, believing that it was his to bring home as he had signed for it. I'd heard reports of Ghanaian soldiers left behind at Beirut airport when weight on the aircraft was an issue—they'd to look after themselves for a week; find somewhere to sleep, food to eat. I knew Ghanaians had been caught deserting, but if some had been abandoned at the airport, well, it's not an impossible scenario. Certainly, the ordinary Ghanaian soldier was treated in a bad way by his officers. I'd witnessed a female officer speak gruffly and harshly to a batman who had ironed her clothes. He held them in the palms of his hands as she went through each item. He stood rigidly at attention. She said nothing, not thanks, kiss my fat arse, nothing. Grunted something to him as she took the clothes from him, and he saluted. Jesus, she was some cow. She walked by me and looked at me and I looked at her and I wouldn't salute her because I'd removed my beret so I wouldn't have to (custom of the service). I hoped she could read my mind: 'You're some cow.'

If a white man treated a Ghanaian soldier the way some of their own officers did, he'd be accused of racism. Concerning racism, a friend of mine told me that a Ghanaian had gotten as thick as pig shite with him when he handed him a tin of black paint and a Finn a tin of white paint. He argued as to why he hadn't been handed the white paint. But we got our own back.

***

All suitcases in the gymnasium were searched and cleared, but confiscations were few and mainly of UNIFIL foodstuffs. Locked luggage was put to one side until the owners arrived and opened them. Officers resenting the searching of their luggage gave lip, bordering on verbal abuse. Pictorial language as I looked out through the netted window, the gentle hills caught in a broad ray of sunshine, trying my best not to erupt in laughter at a Ghanaian officer's umbrage.

'You cannot open my suitcase. I am a captain,' he said.

'Open it.'

'I will report you – you will be in serious trouble.'

'Open it.'

'You are a disgrace. You should call me Sir.'

I'd already paid respect to his rank about four times.

'Sir. If you don't open your suitcase, I will confiscate it and bring it to MP Coy.'

Sighing and blowing hard he bent down and turned the key in the lock. With the seriousness of a surgeon I fitted latex gloves and said, 'Have you anything sharp in your luggage?'

'No.'

'Anything dirty? Shitty underwear, stuff like that?'

His eyes changed into the slits you'd see in old pillboxes, 'No.'

Gloved hands ploughed through his carefully packed clothing and bits and ends, leaving them in disarray. Maybe next time he wouldn't give so much lip.

Nepbatt rotation searches moved more efficiently—350 suitcases packed to the hilt with Lucky Strike cigarettes ... not a hubble-bubble pipe, robes, tablecloth, olive carvings, T-shirt, or electronic good to be seen. Cigarettes only, for sale back in Nepal.

Close to our own rotation I was tasked with investigating an incident in Norbatt, in the village of Ibl al Saqy. A shepherd had found unexploded shells on the side of a hill the Norwegian battalion used for firing practice, above the Hasbayya River. Norbatt MP's billeted in accommodation near their camp, showed me their pet scorpions in a glass tank, handed me coffee and filled me in on the incident. The shepherd had brought home the live shells and was hammering at them to try and get at the powder. There was a market for such powder. A shell exploded and he lost the sight in his eye. His son, about 8, was also blinded. Both were fortunate to have survived. But the, 'Biscuit is this,' I was told, 'the man had been blinded in the other eye some years ago, while doing the very same thing ...'

World's worst criminals—world's worst ordnance scavenger.

In his little yard off his little house, I smelt the poverty and understood why he would tamper with a live shell if it meant raising his living standard to one of subsistence. I couldn't help but feel for him now that he had no more eyes to lose.

Chapter 12

The leaving of MP Coy in the autumn of 1994 was tinged with anxiety. Mam had called to say Dad would collect me on my arrival in McKee Barracks. It was, she went on to explain, something he wanted to do, a goal he had set for himself. Months after his operation he was up and about, putting together the pieces of his life. Medical tests were ongoing, monitoring his condition constantly. The cancer had stripped him of his old voice but at least he was spared having a voice-box inserted in his throat. His words were distorted and hard to distinguish, impossible when the day wore on and he became tired. For the time being he was restricted to liquid food and his sense of taste was poor. There was pain and discomfort and he was lucid to the fact that he had won a major battle and not the war. These were things Mam told me, for Dad could not. I hadn't heard his voice since McDonagh Barracks on the evening I left for Lebanon.

Journeying home then, the subsequent baggage search, the six hour flight, the waiting about at the airport for the rotation to clear customs and be fixed up with pay is almost totally shrouded in mist. I remember feeling guilty at not being around for Dad, for my mother, in terms of providing emotional support. Well, you can't do it in absentia. Thus far, on two major and vitally important occasions, I'd volunteered myself to the margins! What would I say to my Dad? I knew him. He would not want to speak about his illness. He wasn't the sort. Stoic, uncomplaining, he liked to leave the talking to those who had nothing too substantial to say, while his mind made sense of more important issues.

This carousel of thoughts circled my head as Customs went through the flight manifest and chose randomly the names of soldiers whose baggage they wanted to search. The list was given to the liaison officer to call out over the speaker. Oohs and aahs and oh shit, fuck it, murmurs. The victims proceeded to the customs area while the majority continued to enjoy their tea and biscuits, joined in the queue to see their command's pay officer, a few of them no doubt relieved that the contraband in their luggage was safe from penalties that would have eaten into their money. A soldier received four weeks pay and £150 of his Lebanon money, the balance to be paid later, if indeed there was a balance. Soldiers throughout the six months had an opportunity to allot the earned portion of their overseas money home or elsewhere.

Outside in the dark and misty rain, the baggage party worked tirelessly to load trucks with suitcases, aluminium boxes, kitbags … they would set off from the airport before the battalion proper commenced to grind its way towards barracks. The military buses reined to a halt at the de-bussing area in McKee Barracks and we filtered through the transport workshops, searching for the luggage that'd been laid out in sequence by the baggage party according to the respective colour code of each command: red, blue, green and yellow—Curragh Command baggage tagged with yellow paint or electrical insulation tape, the soldier's number, rank and name.

I was looking forward to seeing Dad—to seeing Bernadette and the boys, too, who were waiting at home for me—but first there was Dad. The knot in my stomach grew bigger and heavier. I didn't quite know what to expect. What sort of physical condition was he in? The fact that he'd driven to Dublin was indication that things with him might not be as bad as I had expected. I love my mother, but if someone loses a toenail she builds the story to a leg. Struggling with my gear to the crash barriers and the waiting crowd, reunions happening all around, I had one eye out for Dad. I saw him then, standing apart from the milling throng, his back to the cookhouse wall, scarved and wearing a cloth peaked cap. Under a helium camp light. He had gone very slight in himself, and was like worn rope. The change in him was awful and I fought to contain my shock. I had prepared myself, formed a picture in my head of what he would look like, but the reality of seeing him in the flesh did not fully correspond with the anaesthetised version of him in my mind's eye. Wreckage. The cancer had sculpted him to a certain point and though there wasn't much facial disfigurement there was enough to let you know it had visited. But as well as witnessing close-up the ravages of his illness, I also saw in him the courage, the mental and emotional strength, that had carried him through this storm in his life. And if he were to impart no other teaching to me other than to accept with fortitude what life throws at you, he will have taught me a lot.

We looked at each other. Two of a kind—neither of us great at talking or versed in the art of small talk—and shook hands.

Leaving the eyes to speak for the heart.

The drive home was awkward in the sense that we couldn't engage in conversation. He said things I didn't understand, things that I said, 'Yeah,' to as I did not want to hurt his feelings. He could have been telling me that I was the biggest twin-engine bollocks that God ever put on earth, and I would have said, 'Yeah.' Agreeing wholeheartedly. We listened to a pirated cassette I'd sent him from the Leb. Garth Brooks filled the silence on the journey.

Dad dropped me off at my house in Brownstown, and carried on home to Kildare. It was dark, the breeze across the Curragh plains cutting at me, carrying the smell of furze to my nostrils. Across the grasslands stood the Curragh Camp, Red Brick City, the flashing light on top of the Water Tower a signal that night-firing was in progress on the rifle-ranges. A green flare broke up the night-sky, illuminating for seconds, in its fading breath the rush of rifle-fire. I walked round the back, by the gable end, and opened the gate. Trudy the crow chaser barked till she heard my voice and recognised it, tail wagging. Opening the door I walked in.

Bernadette and Colin were there to meet me. So were cheese sandwiches and Jaffa cakes, and a kettle steaming at the back of the range. We embraced and hugged and Colin put on my blue beret and wanted to know how many bad lads I'd killed. It was too late for Barry to wait up. This was my fourth time to be away from the lads. In total I would be absent from Colin's life through my overseas travels for three years. Maybe I was going to the well too often? I was perhaps suffering from Leb weariness—the tours of duty were coming too quickly and I was beginning to feel unsettled in myself and questioning my values —a fog was lifting and I was beginning to see that my priorities were arranged in haphazard fashion. Promotion; the career soldier? The gloss of army life was beginning to peel away in huge flakes. Service life began to lose its appeal without there being any singular and significant reason for the drift in my career ambitions.

There is nothing like being 'new' at home—catching up on all the news, slipping back into normality, having a month off in which to adjust to family life, to find your bearings. In my absence, Bernadette had made financial decisions, had the car serviced, done things on her own bat; survived without me. When you're home you see this and in the early days of being home you feel as though you are a cog too many. Experience teaches you this and so you learn to blend in gradually and not muscle in: muscle doesn't work.

I woke in the morning to Curragh sunshine, the blind raised and curtains back. The smell of a fry, a jet's contrail splitting the blue of the sky. The radio on. I saw the improvements in the house, things that the Leb money had done ... and lying there on my back a sudden weariness filled me, like a black cloud had breezed in through the open window and sat on my shoulders. A weighted cloud. And then in the corner of my eye there was a movement. Two-year old Barry in the doorway, wide eyes full of blue, holding his soother in his hands. Eyeing me. He ran, climbed into bed, hugged me and then lay down beside me, not saying a word ...

'That's it,' I told myself. 'I'm not going abroad again.'

CHAPTER 13

In Late 1995 I was approached and asked if I'd like to serve in Cyprus for six months. An out of the blue question that threw me. Apparently the UN had asked the Government to supply Irish Military Police to UNFICYP. I thought about it for a few moments, weighing up aspects of the offer, aware that if I gave a commitment which afterwards I could not honour, it'd be akin to handing someone a knife to put against my throat. I'd holidayed in Cyprus a few years previously, staying in Limassol, where I met John Stalker of the Stalker Report fame, and had an interesting conversation with him. It wasn't too long after his controversial investigation into a suspected shoot to kill policy in Northern Ireland. He'd written a book about his experiences and had appeared on *The Late Late Show*.

'I'll have to know by the morning; Command are waiting on feedback,' the officer said.

'Okay, I'll know by then.'

Okay? My arse. When I told Bernadette she looked at me askance, as though the feathers she thought I sometimes had in my head were coming out through my ears. I wasn't a soldier when we married, and neither did I write short stories. But one of which, my first to be aired, was soon to be broadcast by RTE

Radio 1. It was entitled *Elsa's Shop,* and for me was to be the start of something new and exciting.

'No, you'll be away for Christmas. We couldn't do that to Barry.'

When it came to going overseas Bernadette never actively encouraged me to apply or travel, never said, 'No.' Until now. It rang in my head like a church bell after finding its toll.

I went into work the next morning, broke the news and then thought no more of it until after Christmas when the idea of travelling to Cyprus for a year began to pick up momentum. The year long tour of duty in Cyprus was family accompanied and I thought it would be a good experience for us. Meantime, the admin officer had left the unit.

Depot MPC was a revolving door when it came to officers; a stopping place for officers on their way up or out of the army. Bernadette was pessimistic about my chances of success as much as she was about my chances of promotion within the unit, but if my application panned out she'd be on for travelling.

The CO called me into his office about a week after I'd submitted my application.

'Corporal Malone,' he said from behind his desk, 'I can't recommend your application.'

Now there was a tap to the balls.

'Why not, Sir?'

He looked at a piece of paper on his desk, touched it and said, 'You had a domestic problem before Christmas, and couldn't travel to Cyprus.'

'I'd no domestic problem. I was asked if I wanted to go and I said I couldn't. It was too short a call.'

I was seething but remained very calm. Now family commitments was a domestic problem?

'You see,' he said, 'people are volunteering for overseas and they're not lasting the trip for this reason or that. Some for genuine reasons, others less than genuine ...'

He was right.

His eyebrows touched in deep thought. 'I tell you what. You allow the social worker to speak with your wife and we'll take it from there, okay?'

There was an inch scar across the tip of my tongue from biting on it at this stage. You'd think someone had taken an axe to it.

'I'll mention it to my wife.'

Date omitted: *Diary entry:* I'm thinking. Of lots of fuckin' things. Bernadette will go absolutely fuckin' ballistic—have to go tell her now, she's in the kitchen ...

Bernadette did indeed go ballistic. 'You've been away four times and there's never once been a problem, not once did I ever call them about anything and now you're getting this shit. There's no way a social worker is coming in here ... no way.'

Of course there was a way.

That night I sat down and typed a letter and handed it to Bernadette to read and sign. The contents delighted the mischievous side to her. I then told her what she should consider saying to the social worker when she visited, to pull no punches, to ask if she'd be visiting the homes of officers, NCOs and privates, saying this knowing that the social worker would say that she did not discuss the business of her other clients. 'Because,' Bernadette said, 'If I find out that you haven't, I'll be taking legal action for being isolated and victimised by the army.'

Bull. But you have to let people know that your name isn't Shep and you don't roll over. I knew that all my CO was doing was his job, and I understood that. He'd been told by his superiors to vet his men. He was a professional soldier who made sure that any appointments were the correct ones to make.

A few days later I was beckoned to his office. He said, 'The social worker wasn't too impressed with your wife's attitude ...'

'I can't really blame Bernadette, Sir. You know, she knows there was no reason for her to visit our home.'

'And she wrote a letter to me.'

He waved it at me.

'She must be more aggrieved than I had imagined ...'

Later, having reviewed the situation in depth the CO came into the Orderly Room where I was working at that time, and said, 'I'm going to send you to Cyprus ...'

As it turned out, the position had already been allotted to someone else and the CO, feeling genuinely disappointed for me was to say a week later, 'How about acting sergeant in Naqoura, would you be interested?'

The CO was a good guy who'd never let his men down. I appreciated the offer.

A summer trip.

'I'll have to ask my wife.'

'Do that.'

I got the go-ahead and we made plans for the family to holiday in Israel for a week but this didn't pan out for a variety of reasons.

CHAPTER 14

It was a strange and turbulent year. The Israelis set out to break Hezbollah, the fighting so intense, so vicious, that apart from creating havoc and lunacy in a country not unfamiliar with havoc and lunacy, it delayed the outgoing chalks by a week. Watching the battles on the portable TV in our kitchen, Barry, four years old, said, 'That looks dangerous.'

From the mouths of babes …

23 Mar: *Diary entry*: It'd only happen to me—losing a chance to work in Cyprus and ending up working in a country being bombed to kingdom come.

The fighting escalated. Lebanese villagers in the south of the country evacuated their homes, heading north in their droves to Beirut. Katyusha (Little Kate – a Russian name) rockets landed in Israel's northern territories of Metulla and Kiryat Shemona. In retaliation Israeli warplanes attacked Beirut, bombing and strafing its electric generators, plunging the national grid into blackout. Israeli warships blockaded the ports. Hezbollah training camps in the Bekaa Valley were sundered by warplanes that broke the sound barrier passing over Naqoura, the boom like an

Right: After several unsuccessful applications, I finally got a chance to serve abroad for the first time in 1985/86, as a Military Policeman.
© *Author's private collection.*

Left: Sitting at the hippodrome in Tyre with Abou Harb, who was in charge of an army of Amal boy soldiers.
© *Author's private collection*

Right: As well as Irishbatt, we had to work with soldiers from Finland (Finbatt), Norbatt (Norway), Ghanbatt (Ghana), Nepbatt (Nepal), Fijibatt and Frenchbatt.
© *Author's private collection*

6-43

HEADQUARTERS
89
IRISHBATT

IRELAND

Above: Tibnin, 1992. This is a place on a knife-edge of tension. At the time of writing, it was yet again suffering relentless shelling by Israeli forces, in retaliation for Hezbollah rockets being fired across the border.
© *Author's private collection*

Above: My wife Bernadette and new-born son Barry in 1992, just after I had returned home from my tour of duty.
© *Author's private collection*

Above: It was back to work in 1994, where I ended up in places like Tel Aviv, Netanya and Metulla, with a team made up of several nationalities.
© *Author's private collection*

Below: I stopped for the inevitable tourist shot near Bcharre, the birthplace of the great philosopher Khalil Gibran.
© *Author's private collection*

Above: Ghanbatt; the MPs from Ghana in Lebanon.
© *Author's private collection*

Right: The Monument of Peace in Lebanon; 10 stories of tanks, armoured vehicles and artillery, ensnared in layers of concrete and sandbags.
© *Author's private collection*

explosion. Apache helicopters unleashed rockets at ambulances ferrying wounded people to hospital. Smouldering wrecks lay in the middle of the road, surrounded by charcoaled corpses. The Israelis called their military campaign, *The Grapes of Wrath* and it was soon to culminate in tank rounds pouring down on Qana, Fijibatt HQ, where civilians had sought refuge from the fighting. In total, 106 men, women and children were massacred. Israeli spokesmen stated that Hezbollah fighters were taking sanctuary in Fijibatt HQ.

Israeli modus operandi regarding hostage taking entailed the shooting dead of the terrorists, even if this meant killing the hostages in the process. This Hell in the Holy Land—the earth thirsty for blood—was sad and peculiar to see. There was so much savagery in a land revered by the world's religious orders and their devotees. Love, understanding and forgiveness are the core messages of most religions, and yet there was so much killing …

What *Grapes of Wrath* managed to do was unite a people behind Hezbollah and not alienate them as Israel had hoped to achieve—Qana galvanised a nation into righteous fury and indignation.

After Qana there was talk of a ceasefire. Things had quietened enough to allow the rotation to proceed.

Into this cauldron I was supposed to march.

'You're still going ?' Bernadette said, over tea in the kitchen.

'Uh-huh,' I said, eyes looking through the window, a mug of unwanted tea in my hands, a cold sore giving me grief.

'It's getting really dangerous.'

'I'll keep the head down,' I said turning to face her.

'Seriously.'

'What do you want me to say?'

'Nothing, I suppose there's nothing you can say.'

Lebanon was where an Irish soldier soldiered. The country lured, attracted, enticed men like me.

***

Leaving home was always the hardest part. Kissing your kids goodbye in the pre-dawn darkness. Looking at your watch a couple of hours after the leaving and knowing that your youngest son is calling your name and the emptiness is spitting back at him. Tell me about it. It's different with people who know where you're going and why. But severing the bond with a four year old—that burned like fuckin' Hell on barbecue night.

6 April: *Diary entry*: Dad's tests results are coming up positive each time, and the relief in him is great to see – he's getting on with things as best he can. Standing at the sink window I watch Barry at play, try to climb on board his brother's bicycle. Colin enters the yard, slam of side-gate in his wake, and helps him onto the saddle. I think of all the ordinary little things I've missed out on with them … I still say to myself: what the fuck are you are at? All this coming and going, is it worth the money, the upheaval? You're trying to conjure up words convincing enough to fool yourself. You tell yourself that you're providing for your family, doing your country a service, enhancing your career prospects with your sacrifice. You try to brew truths for yourself. In the back of your mind there's a whispering voice:

you're running the risk of losing your family, missing out on time with your kids, moments you'll never get back. But you're deaf to the whispers.

I went to Lebanon because I wanted to get away from the awful tedium of barrack life, because the home uniform strangled my spirit ... for reasons I can't find the words to explain. I accept that things happen for which there are no explanations.

In Lebanon, towns I knew well were being attacked. People killed. Faces I'd known, ordinary people I'd spoken to, all caught up in this madness. I was angry at the Israelis and angry at the Hezbollah. The Israeli response to the Hezbollah attacks was vicious and drew world condemnation. I wondered if the Israeli attack on Qana had been hoped for and planned by the Hezbollah resistance fighters. They know their enemy and thus their response to provocation. Dead civilians are good propaganda for galvanising national and international support. The UN was a neutral force but Israeli heavy-handedness would have at times tested that neutrality. The Israelis were occupying another nation's territory—a strange situation for Irish soldiers in the sense that foreign troops occupied part of our own country ... small wonder perhaps that some Irish soldiers had a sneaking regard for the Lebanese and their cause.

★★★

I left at 4.30am on a Tuesday morning, saying goodbye to Colin and Barry. Colin was up, bleary-eyed, to mind the house for the five minutes Bernadette would be away. Barry was asleep. When

I pushed in his door the light from the landing lay a path to his bed, the breeze stirred the feathers in his dream catcher. I left a present at the foot of his bed, something to take the sting out of my immediate absence. Up and down the country other soldiers were doing or already had done the same thing. Bernadette drove me the short journey to the Curragh camp. We sat awhile in the dark recesses of the square, the engine humming, warming the interior. The radio played soft music.

'This can't go on,' she said, quietly.

'What can't?'

She shot me a sidelong glance that told me to get real. Not to play dumb.

'You've only to say that's it, and I'll pull off the trip.'

'That has to be your decision.'

'Well, I want to go.'

'What are you achieving by this … like, what the hell are you running away from?'

The windscreen was streaked with dirt. The rubber blade on a windscreen wiper was loose, caused by letting the wipers run over frost.

'I'm not running away from anything. The money comes in handy, doesn't it?'

'Get yourself a part-time job and stay at home.'

'You're not making this easy.'

'I'm tired of making it easy.'

Tension strained the cord of muscle in my neck. She was right. I sighed a long sigh that is the language of a soul in distress.

'If things were quiet out there …' I said, 'what do you think it would look like now, eh, if I cried off?'

'Who cares what they think?'

'It's what I'd think of myself that matters.'

We lapsed into silence. By now the buses to bring us to Dublin had pulled into the square and parked in front of the long veranda, lengthy frames shivering in the chill air. Stars beaconed in a sky beginning to dilute its inky colouring.

Bernadette said, 'Make this the last one. Right?'

'Right.'

We kissed and said our goodbyes. I stood and watched the car's red light disappear around a bend, wondering what else was disappearing. I dug my hands deep into the comfort of pockets in my combat jacket and walked to the dining complex. For the first time the blue beret felt like a stone weighing heavily on me.

The motorway was quiet as we travelled towards Dublin airport, almost as quiet the bus itself, where deep thoughts rested on silent tongues. A laziness about the countryside, a serenity, a texture of different greens on the hills rising to the Wicklow Mountains. My eyes drank the landscape; a magpie, then another …

Walking the apron, among the last troops to board the Saint Brigid, a gleaming airbus, I'm thinking of home and Bernadette, if I were being fair to my family, if the investment in my career would pay off? What did I want? Promotion, of course. Not to sit still on the fence. I wanted a successful career. I didn't know it then, of course, but things were already in train that would lead to my career being stalled, effectively and legitimately so.

★★★

The airbus was comfortable, unlike the Boeing 737s used in the 1980s when condensation dripped on us like raindrops falling from trees. For some the five hour flight was torture—time spent smoking their fingers—the plane now a no smoking area. The hostess smiled and said, 'There are smoke sensors in the toilets.'

Nearing Beirut the Saint Brigid banked to the right. In the distance shafts of sunlight chased shadows from the snow-capped Chouf Mountains. Scraps of white cloud in otherwise clear blue skies. Translucent inshore waters revealed coral reefs. A vein of sandy beach put me to mind of dead dogs rotting on the beach at Tyre, a stone's throw from the ruins of the Crusader church—glossy skinned children playing close-by, scuba divers slipping off the side of the boat into the water, searching the sea floor for antiquities, brought there by earthquake and coastal erosion. Wheels bounced on the runway, the plane thundering along, finally shuddering to a halt.

Walking the tarmac in a column of three, we passed burnt-out hangars, and bullet peppered military helicopters. The troops we were replacing were hidden from view in the depths of a hangar. We boarded buses and waited, the sun hot through the grimy windows. The Polish drivers quiet and sullen. Presently, the homeward bound soldiers marched to the Saint Brigid, their relief palpable. Smiles and shouts and cheers from them. Free. Home. A week delayed … all yours now, boys. Welcome. Best of war shit for you, my friend.

Hassan Fawaz spotted me and came over. He was the interpreter from 1992 in Gallows Green. A strain marred his features and in his brown eyes a soft sheen of worry and near despair. 'Murt,' he said, 'ahlan wa sahlan. Again? You almost Lebanese now …'

We talked.

He said, '… My house was hit on the second day but thank the God my family is safe.'

Hassan's house was on a hill on the winding and steep road to Total, within view of the SLA compounds. I'd lunched in his home a couple of times and drank shi, tea, with his family. He knew people who'd been killed in Qana, but the time for grieving had not yet arrived.

His hair had greyed in the intervening years and there was now hopelessness in his eyes. The other wars, the hostilities, had been expected, but this conflagration was not. Lebanon was progressing, people in the south were enjoying peace. Now it is a case of beginning at scratch. I thought of how Hassan and the Lebanese supported the Hezbollah, lauded them as resistance fighters and if they had ever stopped to consider and evaluate the consequences of giving such support to an army that was not the Lebanese army, but one financed by Syria and Iran with no intention other than orchestrating the destruction of the Jewish state. Is it a case of he who rides a tiger being too fearful to dismount?

I watched the Saint Brigid race down the runway, climb high over the Mediterranean, and arc left. Then, minutes later, our 34 vehicle convoy ground along a dirt track, leaving by the 'tradesman' entrance from the airport, passing a rich crop of anemones, scarlet flowers, and Lebanese army artillery positions, sandbagged and canopied with camouflage nets.

On the outskirts of Beirut we gathered speed. Not much sign of any collateral damage. A refugee village, plastic-sheeted tent, brown puddles here and there, displaced people trying to make the most out of what little they had. The smell wafted in to the buses, but when it was long gone, the sight remained clear and distinct. This wasn't a scene of a natural disaster but one caused by war. And I remembered the empathy I had felt for the Jews in the Holocaust museum, seeing those blurry pictures of naked people running to their grave, the panoply of a Nazi empire: Nazi daggers, Iron Crosses, uniforms, SS peak caps, scale models of concentration camps, Swastika banners, viewing footage of the war and the survivors in the camp, the heaps of dead bodies—all that had touched me—and now the Jews were doing the same as the Nazis; displacing people, killing innocents of all ages. It is decent and proper to honour the memory of your fallen, but it is a travesty to behave like those who have given you reason to remember.

**

The further south we travelled, the emptier the roads got. South of Sidon there were no streetlights. Night-time was a canvas of darkness. It seemed as though even the stars were afraid to show. An hour earlier an Israeli gunboat raked this road with heavy machine gun fire. Monkey junction was empty of the monkey seller and his live animal stock, the pumpkin trader gone too. Reaching Tyre, the part of the convoy bound for service in the hills branched away, the remainder, heading for Naqoura and UNIFIL headquarters linked up with the French SISU (SISU is the name of the Finnish company that manufactures armoured personnel carriers) APCs, and continued along the coastal road. Charlie Swing-gate was closed and we were kept waiting for some time as the Fijians liaised with the Israelis to grant permission to cross over.

A pilotless drone hummed in the sky, spying and photographing the landscape, the noise akin to that made by a petrol lawn mower.

Eventually we got the all clear and the convoy moved tentatively through the series of gates. Charlie Swing-gate was a dangerous place, always alive with tension, within scope of attack from AE's. Passing through it, well, you were in a highly vulnerable position. You always felt as though you were in someone's sights. Over the hill, the cliffs next to us, the sea far below, the lights of Naqoura appear …

This was to be my home.

★★★

I bunked that night in Camp Tara with Lester Piggot. It was another Lester, not *the* Lester. He was a nice fella. He talked me to sleep. The next day I moved into MP Coy, sharing a room with a Polish MP called Adam. I'd worked with Adam in 1994 and others whom I knew from that time were also around; Epeli, Seru of the burnt chickens in Metulla that even the cats scudded from. The reports from Qana were worse when heard from eyewitnesses. Some of the soldiers' eyes were dimmed, as if the lights in their souls had been snuffed out.

Considering the soldiers, it did not take a huge stretch of the imagination to ponder the effects this latest campaign was having on the Israeli and Lebanese people. When our tour of duty was complete we were out of the war zone but they had to endure this sort of thing everyday of their lives. It is part of their lives—surviving war.

CHAPTER 15

The next morning I was sitting under the bamboo veranda outside the MP Club, staring out to sea. There's something about the sea I find soothing, peaceful, uplifting. I like to watch the waves lapping to shore, the break of the foam against the rocks: The smell of salt in the air, sometimes heavily scented when the wind combs the waters. The setting sun touching the horizon as though submerging beneath the waves, the stillness when it has disappeared, the moments before darkness. The tea made from the water in the *Burco* boiler, tasted of lime. I was thinking: you're here now, no point in moping, get on with things. I was feeling a little sorry for myself, thinking that I was a sort of shithead for leaving my family so many times. They were growing tired of my absences. I felt numb, too, a little tired. Nothing was new to me anymore. The freshness that had made me an effective and enthusiastic Military Policeman was now almost threadbare. Perhaps I had seen, heard and got to know too much about UNIFIL. The latest crisis had shown how worthless the organisation was as a military force. The Hezbollah and the Israelis had little regard for UNIFIL—a eunuch force. Humanitarian Aid, yeah, alright, but that wasn't why we were meant to be there. UNIFIL, I thought, was a phoney; a peacekeeping outfit who couldn't keep the peace. I looked around the club, at the MP photographs, sipped at my coffee, shifting my thoughts elsewhere, from home, from family. Bolstering myself.

Suddenly, a loud bang, and a whoosh of water spraying upwards from the sea about 100 yards away shook me alert. The noise was loud enough for me to dismiss the notion that the local fishermen were using explosives to kill fish. This was different. A Katyusha rocket had landed in the sea. A week previously, one had impacted 200 yards north of MP Coy, just off the road verge. No casualties, no damage, just a crater left as a reminder and the metal fragments of the rocket.

Stalin's forces had used these rockets to withering effect in World War II. While they were notoriously inaccurate and outdated, they remained potentially deadly. The Hezbollah weren't trying to attack the UNIFIL, their target was the Israeli border, but if we got in the way, Inshallah, God willing. In another word: Tough.

***

Adam's billet was spotlessly kept. His roommate had gone to Beirut on detachment and wouldn't be back for a month. In a week I would be billeted in Patrick Street, as soon as the last of the old Irish had flown home.

The Poles had washing machines. Jesus, I thought, the Irish have been coming here for years. Talk about being last off the blocks. In fairness to us, though, it only took a few minutes to hand wash your clothes and a few minutes for the sun to dry them. If you wanted, all it cost was a couple of dollars to have Fatima in Mingi Street wash and iron them for you. I was a strong supporter of the local economy.

In the coming days of that trip a ceasefire deal was due to come into effect at 4am. Close to 1am on the designated night a rash of Katyushas cut loose over our base, impacting north, well away, but because these rockets were liable to come at intervals we hurried to the bunkers. MP Coy had two bunkers, one modern, the other fifth world, under the MP club, a pisspot of a tunnel, a coal shaft. In the modern bunker on benches arrayed against the walls sat a couple of Finns, and Poles, the fastest runners in the company. All quiet, disturbed from sleep. The bomb shelter was whitewashed and speckled red where mosquitoes had been smacked to death. After a few minutes we ventured outside. Cicadas chirped a maddening chorus. I saw the moonlit walls of the Moorish keep in the Muslim cemetery, a breeze carrying the aroma of burnt mint leaves, a custom here in Lebanon, to burn them as an offering.

The danger had passed.

★★★

Within a fortnight we had our full complement of personnel: Joe Gartland from the Curragh bunked with me, and also on that trip were Capt Gerry Scully, Admin Officer, Lt Col Niall Graham MP Coy CO, Corporals Sinead Byrne and Tracey Walsh, Sergeant Gary Quigley, CS Jim Kelly, CS Mullins and CSM Phil O'Neill.

In Mingi Street I headed towards Ali's to renew acquaintances. I'd just left Ata, the hair stylist who wore tight lilac shorts and a yellow tank-top. Ata handled hair with care unlike the UNIFIL barber who anyone with sense wouldn't let trim a privet hedge. Ata talked of girlfriends, meaning boyfriends, and the life and the swimming, and how the Hezbollah chased him out of Sidon. He used to have two hair salons. Two! he repeated, like he couldn't believe it himself.

'And now look! A little place like this. It makes me want to cry.'

I'd recently upgraded to a notebook that a colleague in work sold me. Ali still flogged electrical goods but was moving into household wares. When I'd entered the shop he was watching television with tears in his eyes. I felt that I'd walked in on him at a bad time. He patted the seat beside him and said, 'Welcome, sit, sit ...'

He shook my hand and let go of a sigh he'd been nursing. Ali was about 60, with large intelligent eyes and had a softness in his features, indicative of a rich, compassionate nature.

Lebanese TV was carrying live coverage of the funerals of the Qana massacre. Coffins draped in the Lebanese flag—red and white with the Cedar centrepiece— being interred in the grounds of the Hippodrome at Tyre, the Byzantine City of the Dead: the acres of sarcophagi; the Roman Arch of Triumph; the flagged way that 2,000 years ago was the road that led into the city... the ancient rostrums under which Abou Harb and his boy militia lived. The Israelis didn't bomb the Roman road or the ruins, so these are still intact.

Ali's forefinger dried a tear on his cheek. 'Always the children suffer. Always,' he reiterated.

He beat his breast small thumps and shook his head.

Coverage shifted to ongoing funerals elsewhere.

Qana. Whole families wiped out. A Fijian soldier running with a child under his arm during the shelling turns to see he is carrying a headless body.

Body parts everywhere. Weeks later a head was found in a tree outside the walls of the camp. A Fijian MP called Chuck, built like a house, showed us photographs he'd taken of the incident: a woman burned black as she sat, her robe a stiff framework, she melted inside. Think of the *Lord of the Rings* movie and the black wraiths on horseback and you'll get the picture. He had a photo of a boy of about eight being zipped up in a body bag. There were many photos of dead and injured bodies, the images graphic and horrifying. Chuck carried them about in his pocket as though they were a deck of cards. I looked at him and wondered. I told Epeli he had to watch out for him, because Chuck was showing us the pictures in his head.

A newspaper report carried a story of a boy mistakenly thought to have been killed in the shelling, who had been placed in a body bag and left … stories upon stories to chill the marrow.

A truce was held. Refugees returned to their villages, many to homes damaged beyond repair, and spent the summer salvaging and sorting out a place to live before the winter arrived.

After Ali's and a beer, I looked at the family photos …

20 April: *Diary entry*: Why are we here? What's the UN about if it can't stop all this killing, this destruction of property? The Blue Beret—the UN flag—it means nothing to people intent on destroying each other. All the UN is doing is bearing testament, witness, to what's going on and giving as much

humanitarian aid as possible to those in trouble. But we're not fulfilling our mandate: to help the Lebanese Government re-establish its authority in the south, to oversee the Israeli withdrawal to the internationally recognised frontier. Well, the Hezbollah are part of the Lebanese Government and are intent on wrestling control of the region from the Israelis. They don't need our help.

We're pig in the middle and can't do a thing to prevent innocent people being used as pawns by both sides in the war. As a force we aren't strong enough to do what should be done, to prevent the fighting. We shouldn't be here, I think, it's time to move on. We're not fuckin' wanted, instead of finding a solution to the problem we have become part of the problem.

CHAPTER 16

P hil O'Neill assigned me to work in the Provost Section, under a Polish staff officer called Stanley, who wore a handlebar moustache, the corners of which seemed to pull down on his face and give it a craggy look. I was working as a shift commander in the duty room situated at the Company's exit/entry point. This was the heart of the company, where the duties for the border reported in, personnel signed their weapons in and out of stores, the out book if they were heading into the AO or to Israel for the day. A repository for information and the holder to the keys of the cells and the armoury. Keeper of the daily journal.

We worked a Scandinavian civilian police system: 3pm to 11pm; 7am to 3pm; 11pm to 7am; rest day, off day. There were undertones of disquiet among the Fijians but particularly the Norwegians at how Stanley operated the duty roster. They alleged that he was showing favouritism to his own nationality when it came to weekends off. A close scrutiny of the roster didn't declare any glaring discrepancies of this nature. I knew from home service that there were times that a duty roster lost the run of itself and certain people were screwed for duties while others appeared to get a handy run, though, I think things balanced out in the end. The person making the detail has to allow for leave, sickness, courses, unexpected tasks, exercises, and such like, and the ship of fairness for an individual can traverse choppy waters for a while. It also has to be said that a duty roster can be used to screw someone who might be considered in need of a good screwing i.e. a slap across the wrist instead of being formally charged. Or spite, or vengeance, or just out of sheer dislike—a person preparing a roster might be open to temptation arising from these human failings and abuse his position. For example he might send six Military Police to conduct a search at 4am to the amazement of the requisitioning officer who'd asked for two. The Norwegians, I'd noticed, and it was present in a small way in 1994, and not at all in 1985/1986, had nurtured resentment towards the Irish appointments in MP Coy. The Irish, they contended, held most of the key appointments. The attractive ones. This was true: The Commanding Officer was Irish, so too the Deputy CO, Pay Officer, the Crime Reader, there were also Irish in SIS and Traffic.

Norwegians held positions in Traffic and SIS, but they'd more MPs serving in the company than the Irish, and it wasn't unusual for highly trained and high ranking civilian police officers to spend their working hours on checkpoint duty and searching luggage at the border, duties they would have by virtue of their home status thought beneath them. Occasionally a couple of them aired their grievances to me, and I'd get thick and say, 'I've only got three stripes and one of those has been lent to me, I can't help you.'

They'd shrug and say, 'Yes, but this is not fair. It is a problem.'

'Fine, but it's the Irish who polish your reports before you submit them to the Crime Reader, yeah? And it's he who'll correct them further.'

'The secretary does that.'

'So, you want the Crime Reader position? I think the force commander himself would object to that.'

There was a mixture of civilian Norwegians and civilian police, and it was mainly the civilian police who moaned. They probably had a point. The thing was, I suspect, there just wasn't the work in UNIFIL for them to bring their talents to the fore. Scene of crime investigation and preservation? Irish Military Police were invariably trained by the Gardaí in their Forensic HQ at the Phoenix park on a six to eight-week course. Home investigations honed fingerprinting skills, crime scene photography, sketching, so we were on a par with the Scandinavians and the average Irish garda in this regard.

I learned a lot from the Norwegians though, and I liked being in their company when they weren't telling me how shabbily they were being treated. They supplied two drug dogs to the company along with their handlers. In Norbatt there was a dog platoon and a pet cemetery. None of the dogs was allowed back into Norway after service in the Middle East. Their kennels were air-conditioned, not for their comfort but to preserve their sniffing powers. The handlers themselves were pleasant and easy to work with and had a great rapport, as you'd expect, with their charges.

The dogs were useful in the sense that they were a deterrent. Often they'd pick up a scent of cannabis, where it had been smoked or carried in a bag. Once, a dog named Prince went wild and started to bark and paw at a locker in the French lines, but there was nothing inside except a salami sandwich gone green and mouldy.

★★★

The one thing I learned on that trip was that conventional armies couldn't beat insurgent armies. They find it well-nigh impossible to defeat a guerrilla army engaged in snipe attacks. History teaches us this lesson time and time again. What Ireland should have done at the outset of independence was to understand the nature of combat that won it freedom and therefore to be original in its defence policy, i.e. to have a standing guerrilla army so to speak, and a regiment for other duties, including ceremonial. We see Iraq as a classic example: the Americans won the initial ground campaign but it's finding it impossible to prevent its soldiers being killed fighting against an army of shadows.

Hezbollah was a guerrilla outfit that the world's top army couldn't break.

★★★

During that tour, we had a prisoner. A Jordanian, Khamis Khodr, PLO member, who had been in an Israeli prison for 23 years. In the 1960s as a young fighter in Yassar Arafat's PLO, he crossed the Jordan river to attack Israelis and ended up being arrested. He wasn't wanted in Israel nor in Lebanon, so UNIFIL took him on board and he lived in a cell in the duty room, using another as a kitchen. He was dark-skinned, wiry, with grey in his hair. 57, but looked older. He pottered about MP Coy doing this and that whenever the mood took him, kept the rockery under the unit's flag pole free of weeds. The Red Cross visited him, bringing food, parcels of clothes and money gifts.

The PLO paid him a salary, too—not much, and it didn't always arrive when supposed to. He liked his beer and his cigarettes and made friends with a couple of the Irish MPs. He liked to sit under the frangipani tree opposite the duty room and smoke cigarettes and boil water for tea on a little gas ring. I'd see him sometimes stare north east across the sea at Tyre, the tower blocks white in the dazzling sun, and sometimes he'd fix his eyes south at the cliffs, and I'd know he was thinking of Palestine—he called it Palestine. He winced whenever he heard young Military Police say they were crossing into Israel on leave.

***

Promotion for me within the Irish army was like being on a treadmill. You worked toward it but got nowhere and earned nothing except a good sweat. Frustrating for the career soldier, the soldier for life, which I wasn't too sure I wanted anymore.

It was an interesting anomaly that an acting sergeant when on detachment and overseas service was put in charge of ranks much higher than his, had this responsibility entrusted upon him, yet at home he was put in a box and proverbially beaten across the head when it came to the promotion race, told that seniority counted for a lot when it came to promotion. Stymied on the home front, a stonewalled career, frustration seeped in until I made up my mind that it didn't matter and when I did this, I was no longer frustrated. I still applied for vacancies but just for the sake of it. In most instances a glance down the candidate list would apprise me of the successful applicant.

The army, see, like I've said, mirrors society. I began to take the army *cum grano salis;* with the proverbial pinch of salt. In comparison to other countries, it galled me to see and hear other soldiers speak of when they could expect promotion. They had a career path, a promotion path—do their job, pass the courses and it was a given they'd be promoted. It stands to reason. One of my biggest regrets, because it proved a complete waste of time, was to undergo a 12 week standard course to qualify for promotion. I finished 2nd in the course placings but years down the line I was still a corporal with no sign of promotion in the pipeline. Overseas missions opened my eyes to how badly treated the Irish Military Police man was in this regard. For someone like me, there was nowehere to go.

***

Nahariya was my first detachment posting in 1996. The lease had run out on the old MP detachment and was not renewed. Instead the detachment was located in a poky basement flat, combining office, bedroom, kitchen and bathroom in the large OGL Recreation House or Rec House. It was situated next to the beach, not far from Jabotinsky Street and the old detachment. The basement was a dirty kip, no matter how well we cleaned it. A solid manifestation of how the recent budgetary cutbacks affected UNIFIL's operations. The strength of MP Coy had been reduced and the food allowance for detachments in Lebanon withdrawn. In Israel, the allowance was now $23 a day, and as usual was paid in retrospect of service. Two MPs comprised the sum strength of the detachment, sleeping head to toe in mosquito netted bunks. The duties involved investigation of traffic accidents, the illegal parking of UN vehicles and escorting UNIFIL troops across the border at the regulated late crossings of 6pm and 11pm. The Israeli liaison officers were of diverse nationalities. One Dub in the Israeli Army frequently asked if there were any copies to hand of *The Sunday World*. Newspapers from home arrived to MP Coy about a week old.

The liaison officers were strict about timings and no baggage or personnel was allowed cross the border from Lebanon into Israel after 6pm unless by prior arrangement. We didn't count the days in Nahariya, just the late crossings. Each MP had 63 to get through. 21 days.

When I arrived at the Rec house I shook hands with Yves Babin, a French Gendarme. Slinging my bag under my bunk it was met with resistance and a loud clink of glass. Dropping to my hunkers to see the cause of the blockage, I found a treasure hoard of vodka and whiskey bottles and cartons of cigarettes, the floor under the bed taken up with them.

'Yves, what's this?'

Yves shrugged and ran a hand over his tight brown hair. He had aquiline eyes and a well groomed moustache.

'It's the Polish,' he said, pulling a face, shrugging his shoulders.

'You're not serious?'

A couple of smuggling runs like this paid for holidays and other expenses, thus preserving their home pay.

I thought: What the fuck should I do? Confiscate and report?

Why should I do that when Yves hadn't? Not alone would I walk the Polish MPs into the stew but Yves would have his knuckles rapped too. When I was considering my options a Polish MP arrived in, whom I knew, smiled and said, 'Not to worry. I will take this stuff out, now ...'

This carry-on was normal. Once, when checking Polish baggage during one of their rotations I was approached by a Polish MP who pointed at a row of 10 identical bags and asked me not to search them, '... they are for customs at home.'

Admittedly, I had a natural reticence about reporting my own. In addition there would have been a backlash against me if I had spoken up, plus I believed the smuggling between the Poles was so endemic that it didn't really matter whether or not I acted on this particular instance. It wouldn't have made a difference, not in the larger scheme of things. I didn't like the idea of the corruption, and I didn't smuggle ... if others wanted to run the risk of being caught then let them. Sometimes you have to turn a blind eye—if you don't, you get snowed under.

***

Food; we fended for ourselves. Some days I crossed the border and dined in the international mess, though not entitled to since I was in receipt of food money. I was Dogface Nahariya, in spite of there not being much to be dogface of. I liked to foot patrol the town in the morning, arriving back about noon, always carrying a Motorola, a hand held radio. In a shop called Doron's I might buy a novel and a couple of periodicals. Usually, I borrowed my books from a UNIFIL Library in Naqoura. A haunt of mine. I posted letters home from Israel and used the French Post office in Naqoura, in addition to the Irish postal system, just for the sake of change and convenience rather than any personal preference. There was a time that the Irish were allowed to send parcels home at no cost, but this practice was phased out for one reason or another.

Things in the shops were a shade dearer than at home; a Big Mac, chips and cola in a McDonalds wedged between shops at a bus depot cost 19 shekels, roughly $6.50. 1996 prices, three shekels to the dollar. Yves rarely went on foot patrol. He sat on a chair outside the kennel and basked in the sun, listening to music. Resting himself was something he had down to a fine art.

In the MP Mess in Naqoura, Phil told me about an incident. Chuck of the Qana photographs flipped and wrecked the MP Club. He had brushed Polish MPs aside as though they were flies and again, it was Epeli who settled an issue by saying a few words. Chuck came away with him like a lamb. This news passed on to me a few moments before a call came over the Duty room tannoy: 'Phone call, Sergeant Malone, phone call, Sergeant Malone …'

One thing a soldier hated to hear in UNIFIL was his name sounding over the tannoy. It was okay if a call was expected, but an unexpected call—well, only one thought floods your mind: is everything all right at home?

I crossed in front of the line of MP Coy transport, pushed in the steel blue door and took the blue phone across the counter from Sami Navivilu—Sami's a tough nut—a prison ink tattoo on his upper shoulder, 'F-ck,' and underneath, 'All that's missing is U.'

'Hello, Murt here.'

This accent came back at me, polished, refined, articulate, 'Hi, I'm Pam Brighton from BBC Radio 4. It's about a short story that you submitted, *Dream Horse*, we'd like to use it.'

Naturally, I was thrilled. Bernadette had told Pam of my whereabouts and had given her UNIFIL's switch number.

'Pam, I'm delighted. Sure, go ahead, of course.'

'Yes, but I'd like another 400 words, five, even.'

'Oh.'

Pam faxed the story over and I worked the night long on it and faxed it back to her through the UN. Brilliant. I was making inroads into the writing world. My first story had been broadcast on RTE in May. Bernadette had sent the cassette and I'd listened to it in Nahariya. Joe Taylor, the reader, was later to cut a name for himself re-enacting court scenes from a major tribunal. But *Dream Horse* and the BBC! It meant that more than one producer liked my work. I was doing something right. When I told the lads they were delighted about it and asked what it was about. Then we went back to talking about Chuck.

Across in Nahariya the following day I got it into my mind and drove to Akko. Yves had been replaced by Ness Romau, a shaven headed, barrel- chested Frenchman. He introduced himself to me as, 'The new Nahariya Beach Boy,' and promptly headed off to the sandy ways with a beach towel under his arm, sunshades fitted, smelling of coconut oil. The noise of his flip-flops receding ...

'Ness,' I called.

He turned about, the sun glinting off his gold neck-chain, 'Yes.'

'Bring a Motorola with you.'

He slapped his forehead with the flat of his hand, 'Fuck! Sorreeee, my friend. Of course.'

And then he patted what he called his mosquito airport, his bald pell, and added, 'Merde!'

Some general's wife sitting at a picnic bench cut him in two with a dagger look.

'Sorreee,' he said to her, laughing at her reaction and not in the least bit sorry at all. He was loud, opinionated but very likeable.

Akko, ten kilometres south of Nahariya, was another place on our patrol beat, or used to be. In a tiny front garden stood huge chocolate coloured topped mushrooms, polka dot stems. I suppose it made a change from the ubiquitous palm trees. Parking the minibus at the foot of a series of steps leading to the battlemented sea walls, I set off on foot along the wall, heading towards Burj al- Kommander, a squat bastion tower in the north-east corner of the old city, that afforded a panoramic sweep of the bay and Haifa port and city. I climbed down and walked the narrow streets, passing the crusader church of St John, the copper shops, a jewellery shop where I bought an 18 carat gold Jerusalem cross and chain for Bernadette, on to Ottoman square, where cavalry horses used to be stabled. Al-Jazzar Street was next and the mosque bearing the same name. Al-Jazzar mosque stands on the site of a former crusader cathedral. Outside the mosque a seller of fresh orange juice came round the side of his stall and said, 'Your boots I like very much – will you give me your boots?'

'And what'll I wear?'

He thought on this and said, 'My sandals.'

Scuffed and worn, fit for the dump they'd been scavenged from.

'No, thanks.'

'Next time you come back, bring me the boots, yes?'

'Sure.'

'I live on the beach,' he said. He pointed to his eyes and said, 'I see my wife with the other one and I kill her. That is why I am here. I used to be rich.'

He said he was Italian, and breathed 'Dio grande,' a lot, which proved nothing really. I bought a juice from him and said I'd bring him a pair of boots.

'Dio grande,' he said, or something like it.

Across the street from the Al-Jazzar is the entrance to the subterranean Crusader city, a haunting series of vaulted halls, crypts beneath modern Akko. The crusaders lost the city to the Mamluks in the late 13th century and the quarter I stood in was once the dining area of the Knights Hospitaller. A passing tour guide breathes that Marco Polo is mentioned in chronicles as having stayed here many times.

You get a feel for places like Akko. Ruins are a throwback to times past. Give you as much to reflect upon as the stars. The ephemeral nature of life. Text written on marble, at the effigy of a dead knight, read, 'In the year 1242 after the incarnation of Our Lord, the XV15 KLS of October, passed away Brother Peter de Villebrede, eight Grandmaster of the Hospitallers...'

Another inscription in Latin reads—obviously the city was close to capture at this stage—'Passers-by, pray for my soul ...'

I went back a couple of times to Akko, said a prayer for the soul and brought canvas boots along for the juice seller, but he and his cart were nowhere to be seen.

12 June: *Diary entry* ... letters from home, drawings sketched by Barry. The call home is funny. As usual Barry insists on being the first to speak with me, and the last. I hear him in the background asking Colin for the phone. Why is that? The first to speak, the last? What's going in that little head?

CHAPTER 17

After I had run out of late crossings I returned to MP Coy and went back to performing Shift Commander duties. Plans were in place to run a Fiji night in MP Coy. The club decorated with fronds resonated with the sound of the kava root being ground to powder, for hours a rhythmic thump-thump. The powdered kava is put on a thin cloth and sieved with water, into a receptacle. A dun coloured substance, it's non-alcoholic but is a potent beverage that tastes of the earth. Ritualistically, a small bowl is handed to you, you clap hands before receiving it and then swallow the kava in one attempt. It is regarded as a very mild narcotic with curative properties. Certainly I found this to be the case as whenever I drank the grog I didn't blink for two-days. Kava hits you from the temples in.

Part of the beauty of serving with MP Coy was the opportunity it afforded to socialise and work alongside other nationalities, learning about their customs, culture, outlook on life and so on. Indeed, in today's Ireland the experience of working with this multi-national force has helped me deal with and understand the foreign nationals who have come to Ireland. I know their problems, the reasons they are here, a little about their national psyche.

A Fijian band played music from the South Seas, and a rendition of the Red, White and Blue, a sorrowful lament. Three of the soldiers wounded in the Qana massacre were present, here but not with it. Sami talked. The bitterness rolled off his tongue, as he listed sotto voce, the extent of their injuries, '... they attacked a UN camp—to murder civilians—why? Qana ... Qana was horrible?'

He was present when it happened, like Chuck.

He handed me a tumbler of grog and after I downed it, we looked at the flickering video images of his homeland on the TV; grass-skirted and barefooted walkers tread across a bed of burning stones ... no pain, no scorch marks on the soles of their feet. Like a wedding video there was only so much I could take and I made my excuses and left. The grog was starting to knock against my temples. I went into the bar to get something to eat from the buffet, another effect of the grog: it enhances your appetite. Then I remembered the squeals of a pig in the dip of wasteland that separated MP Coy from Camp Tara, where aviation fuel used be stored in enormous rubber containers, as the Fijians set about killing it. There were quirky happenings about food in MP Coy. The Nepalese in their billet cooked mussels they'd found on the beach, the Ghanaians were fond of donkey, cat too, I'd heard. I passed on the pork.

When I got home, Khamis, the prisoner, was arguing with the Polish barman. He was tipsy and had been refused drink, but not in a polite way. The barman was new to me. He'd a face like thunder. Disgruntled at working the bar, a job allocated on a fortnightly basis to the different nationalities within the company.

'Khamis ...' I said weakly, unsure of the right tone to adopt with him.

Then Sinead who was on patrol arrived and led Khamis back to the duty room, calmed him down, fed him his cigarettes, diffusing the situation. Not yet 21, she showed throughout her trip a maturity beyond her years and a real common sense approach, always pro-active. Stanley popped in to the cell and assured Khamis that he would have strong words with his man.

'No manners, that man,' Stanley affirmed, saying it like he was hurt for Khamis.

It was more than an absence of manners, and Khamis knew this, but he had come back to himself now and wanted no more trouble.

The next day I ran into John Lynch in the dining hall at Camp Tara during lunch. Camp Tara had become the place to eat as the standard fare in the International Mess was dire. John had fixed up my laptop back in the Curragh, installing additional memory chips. We'd worked together for a period in McDonagh Barracks. John was a wizard with computers and his expertise was always in demand. He made friends in Italair, whose computer system he'd installed, and they'd befriended him. Italair—we called it *Cappuccino Acres* just to indicate its exclusiveness and the fact that cappuccino was their beverage, also like with every military unit there was a little of *them* and *us* ... John had an easy-going and obliging manner about him. His family accompanied him and were staying across the border in Nahariya.

Phil called me into his office one morning. Adjusting his glasses he said, 'Murt, we need an Irish Military Police presence in Beirut. There's an Italian cartel in UNIFIL House that needs to be broken up. You'll be there for two months. Gary will relieve you then. Okay?'

Not really, I thought to myself. I didn't want to go.

UNIFIL House is situated in Bir Hassan, a 20 minute drive from the airport. This five-storey apartment block is the nerve centre of UNIFIL and other UN agencies.

'I've booked you on the heli-flight for tomorrow morning…'

'I'll drive up.'

'Take the helicopter. It's handier.'

'Jesus, I dunno, I hate flying … a helicopter … I …'

'Try it. You'll find it's a great experience.'

I was caught in the middle of a power struggle. The CO, Surb (Senior UNIFIL Representative in Beirut) of UNIFIL House was Italian, so too the pilots stationed in UNIFIL House and one of the MPs, whom Surb liked and did not want to leave for MP Coy. There was a tug of war and the Italian MP lost out. Phil had dug his heels in and insisted that MP Coy control its deployment of Military Police and not an officer from outside the unit.

1 July: *Diary entry:* It's hot. The notion of flying by chopper bothers me as much as the stifling heat. I write a letter, read a little, light a mosquito coil on my bedside locker and lie down on my bunk that is draped with a new mosquito net. A little after 11 pm I'm alone in the room, the bedside light on. Outside there is the noise of someone watering shrubs. I bring a dream on, think of home.

The next morning the patrol dropped me off at the helipad. I looked through the waiting room window at the white Huey, rotor blades cutting the air, engine high-pitched, and thought about fucking off back to MP Coy and pleading cowardice to Phil. But shit, look, I said to myself, 'There's the drug dog and not a bark out of him, and he's flying too. Dogs sense trouble …'

Maybe he's drugged?

I was fitted out with earmuffs and a life vest. Under the wind of the blades we walked, sat where the flight officer indicated, buckled up, the dog giving a little whine in his travel cage, which I thought a portent. If you always think the worst, you're bound to get it right at least once. Right?

The nose of the helicopter tipped forward as we lifted. Off we went, banking right over MP Coy, the Moorish keep, travelling out to sea, riding the coast to Beirut. The co-pilot motioned the pilot to climb higher. *Fuck! Is this a trainee flight?* The heli searched for altitude, shuddering under the effort. Metal straining, nuts and bolts loosening.

Oh sweet divine Jesus … I could see tobacco groves, scrubby hills criss-crossed with goat-trails, the tumuli of ancient ruins in Tyre, mosaic avenue flanked by Cipollino columns leading to the sea. I thought of the sarcophagus of Antipater, its bas-relief of Medusa, the snake goddess, carrying the inscription …'a fisher of Murex,' a snail from which purple dye was derived. I could see the bones of the crusader sea castle in Sidon, by the fish market. Dirty clouds dirtier over distant mountains. Thirty-minutes flying and I'm thinking, 'Hey, this is okay, fine, grand, not so bad.'

I hate flying. I've had nothing but bad experiences. Like when I was flying from Larnaca to Baghdad and I was oh so totally relaxed—I'd worked hard at relaxing. Midway into the flight, over

Iraq's red desert and rocky terrain, we encountered turbulence, and then severe turbulence, and when the stewardess sat in beside me, blessed herself and brought a cross to her lips and kissed it, I imagined the worst. She was sweating, close to panic.

'It's okay,' I said, unconvincingly.

'Normally taking off and landing is the worst.'

'Do you like this sort of work?'

'No.'

'Maybe …'

'Yes, I must get a different job. Everyone says it.'

The Heli.

When we landed, I walked to the MP minibus and shook hands with Yves and Thom, a Norwegian, whose name triggered another Thom I'd known, a guy who'd been sunbathing on the roof at UNIFIL House in 1986 and was shot in the foot for his efforts.

Air-conditioned rooms, large screen TV with CNN, two cooks. Peter, a Pole, was my roommate. He was quiet, hadn't much English, and kept the nail on his small finger long. For fashion? I don't know. Didn't like to ask. Yves briefed me as he showed me around. Our office was two desks and a filing cabinet in a room that faced the Italair desk. This room led into the secretary's office and another that was the CO's. Three bedrooms and a bathroom and toilet.

'Terese,' he said, 'she will ask you not to use too much toilet paper, it blocks up, yes?'

He pushed the handle down. Talk about a weak flush. Spitting in it would have had better effect. In Tyre we had a dry toilet and always had to fill a bucket of water to flush the waste away. That was part of the duty NCO's task, to fill the buckets with water, because if you didn't you could bet that someone, usually a guest, would drop his load and walk away – leaving someone else to spirit away his droppings. Isaac the Ghanaian had forgotten and been terribly affronted by the sight of what he termed, 'Elephant dirt.'

Yves led the way across the corridor to another apartment the same size of the one we'd just left—dining room, kitchen stores, sitting room, conference room, and three more bedrooms.

'Ness is coming tomorrow,' Yves said, 'for the weekend.'

The New Nahariya Beach Boy.

Yves introduced me to Kari-Anne, a Norwegian logistics lieutenant, who often accused me of using her washing powder. I think it was said just as a conversation starter.

***

Traffic in Beirut was chaotic. Cops on motorbikes, under mushroom shaped weather shelters at junctions, endeavoured to keep traffic flowing, but it was a Sisyphean task and sometimes unmanageable. Electric cabling strung across a narrow street were like jungle vines. I half-expected to see Ali of the Apes in action. We didn't carry any weapons in Beirut. In fact UNIFIL troops were not supposed to carry arms beyond the Litani River Bridge outside Tyre. We had pistols; these were secured in a safe in the House. At six the next morning, shortly after first light, Terese the cleaning lady appeared. Like a henna-haired angel of vengeance she coursed through our floor, banging things, complaining to herself in Arabic, no doubt about the mess from the night before, the beer cans, possibly identifying the culprits by the brand of beer and crisp packet.

'No good Irish, no good Norwegian, no good Polish, no good French,' she said, like a mantra.

She was called ,'Four Mothers.'

'Hello?' I said.

'Hello,' she said back, looking at me like I were a mouse in a trap.

She carried on then, bringing the vacuum cleaner into the CO's office. She had a cross face, no doubt. It warned you off, but when you got to know her a little she opened up and you discovered that the cross face wasn't really cross but hurt and anxious. She lived on her nerves.

Rida, the cook, showed next. A tall dark-haired young man whose wife was expecting their second child. He collected fresh bread rolls for the section every morning in the grocery shop down at the bottom of the hill from UNIFIL House. Hamid was our evening cook. He cooked soup.

Rida advised against sending post through the local system, dismissing the notion by lifting an eyebrow and suggesting that the post office at the airport was the ideal solution, '… maybe.'

Then he said, 'What will we have to eat for lunch? Pasta, lasagne?'

Ah, of the Italian mindset.

'Potatoes, chops,' I said, 'for a change.'

I was responsible for filling out the food requisition forms and submitting them to Naqoura. Ensuring that items such as milk cartons that carried a picture of a beautiful Israeli woman and Hebrew writing were discretely packed away in the fridge. If seen by the wrong eyes it could cause a problem. The likelihood of it happening wasn't high, but you did have to spare a thought for Rida, Hamid and Terese. Their country had had the shit hammered out of it by the Israelis, so they didn't want a smiling Jewish face to greet them first thing in the morning. I remember once in Baghdad, a colleague of mine had thoughtlessly said, 'Shalom,' to a Muslim and this young man almost choked to death on the spot from a case of immediate apoplectic rage.

Rida's eyes went like headlamps on full, 'The CO he likes pasta.'

'Surprise him, Rida.'

He didn't, of course. He made two menus.

Cute hoor.

Yves said that last week had been very busy. Kofi Annan, UN Secretary General, had visited Ross Mountain, the American attaché, and the CO had to be escorted here and there. We were the CO's drivers and as UNIFIL's chief representative in Beirut, he was invited to a lot of functions held by the various ambassadors in the city.

In the morning, at about 7am, we had the briefing. The CO sat at the head of the table, an avuncular figure, with a thin grey goatee, and brown eyes that appeared haunted or worried about some past or future event. He was about 60 and while I think that he liked Beirut, he disliked the plethora of diplomatic functions he had to attend. He fretted about little and much. Born worrier as opposed to warrior.

I was introduced to him and the Italian pilot, a gentleman with a gold chain dripping from his neck and wearing a flight-suit. He was never without a smile, his lips like loose knicker elastic. I asked myself how someone who had to drive those metal crates six times a week could be so relaxed and content in himself?

Escort and driving duties aside, Military Police also drove to the airport three times weekly to perform traffic control duties for the UN choppers, to ensure that vehicles remained at a safe distance during the landing. There'd almost been a couple of accidents when this wasn't done, when airport maintenance staff had driven small transporters too close to the landing pad for the pilot's comfort.

'So, Murt,' the CO said, 'you take a car and get used to driving around the city, okay. Frank; you show him the route to the airport and how to get into the city.'

Then he went on to list the events coming up, his driver needs and the like.

The Military Police had two Land Cruisers. When driving the CO, Aldo, we used the transport allotted to him: UNIFIL 5 or 6, Chevrolet Caprice, automatic transmission. I drove Aldo in this once, to Terese's house, as he wanted to extend his condolences to her over the loss of a close relative. A very fat woman sat in the back with him. He forgot that I didn't know the way to the house and several times at the woman's sudden interjection in a soft inaudible voice—for some reason she would not speak directly to me—he said, 'Go this way ... Left here ... Right ...' His tone impatient. I'd had a rough night of it with my tinnitus, which had been getting steadily worse since it first appeared a few years before, when I was out on the firing ranges. I hadn't gotten much sleep and ended up disturbing Peter at three in the morning after I gave up fighting the constant ringing in my ear and got up.

I must have gone into every pothole, every shell-mark in

Beirut, bouncing my passengers. The woman bitched about my driving and he bitched too, and right on cue during one of his mega bitches I hit another hole, the biggest yet. By the time I pulled up in front of a house across from a thin copse of pine, the CO had a fringe he was too busy fixing to reproach me. He said nothing but he never asked me to drive him anywhere again. Indeed, I was restricted to driving the *Caprice* to the wash in a garage where men in rubber boots and overalls earned their crust washing vehicles the day long. I suppose it's not good practice to shake a V.I.P.

To augment the food supply at the house we all bought in our own preferences. *Aoun* Supermarket was well-stocked and I bought in a few cans of Guinness and cooked ham – like, the food from Naqoura, it was yellow-pack stuff and bland.

'Beirut is back,' was the catchphrase of the Lebanese trendy. Discos, night-clubs, restaurants and busy hotels bore testament to the revival. The Green line—a demarcation line that divided Muslim and Christian during the civil war was being re-built. Terry Yorath, the former Leeds and International Welsh soccer player, managed the Lebanese national team. Everywhere demolition of war damaged buildings, the Phoenix like resurrection of others. In all, the reconstruction project would cover an area of 1.6 million square metres, take 20 years to complete and see an investment of $13 billion. Lebanon, you sensed, under the guidance of its wealthy and well-connected prime minister, the recently murdered Rafiq Hariri, would soon be re-acquiring its title as the Riviera of the Middle East. In the same glance you could see the wealth of the country and also its abject poverty. It showed its face along the Corniche Walk, a coastal pedestrian way, a route I used to try and keep the weight in check. In one stride the rich behind fences, sunbathing on a fine sandy beach, and in another a poor woman climbing out from under a building where she and her small child had spent the night. Shades of today's Dublin.

Street vendors hawked their wares of coffee, hot corn on the cob, roasted nuts, bread with a handle, like handbags strung from bicycle handles. Lose the weight! I think I gathered some on those walks.

A normal taxi run from the airport into the city cost about $15. One young Irish soldier told me he'd paid $40. Double prices or more for the unwary.

An old man in a shop, when asked for the price of a child's soldier uniform, told me it cost $30. 45 minutes and two glasses of coffee later I walked out with it underarm for $20. Both of us happy, delighted too at the craic gleaned from the bargaining. As the exchange rate was 1,500 Lebanese pounds to the dollar, the currency was really US$. Who wanted to walk around with a wallet full of thousands of notes that wouldn't buy you a falafel or a cola?

There were posters everywhere, of martyrs and politicians, of Middle Eastern pop stars. Recruitment posters too, I thought, of a youth in camouflage uniform, wearing a red headband and brandishing a Kalashnikov rifle.

One evening, prior to leaving for the Canadian Embassy on escort duty I called home. Barry still owned his obsession: he had to be the first of the family to speak with me and also the last. And the last thing he said to me that evening was this, '... me crying outside for you.'

Then a sob.

Fuck, like.

What do you say to your child when he comes out with stuff like that?

It touched a raw nerve. Bernadette had heard him crying in the garden shed and when asked what was wrong with him, he told her the above. Bernadette and Colin had decided not to tell me, but Barry had other ideas.

The embassy bash ran late, or into overtime, and Yves called the house to say we'd be late in and not to keep dinner for us. Aldo, the CO, when done with the function, approached us and said, 'I need to go to the yacht club, okay. You will get something to eat there ... my treat.'

We're sitting there, outdoors, next to a large swimming pool, yachts rocking in the harbour, being waited upon. Yves did the ordering in French to the waiter.

'Murt,' he said.

'Yeah?'

'Do you know how much it is to be a member of this club? For one month?'

'No idea.'

'$2,000.'

'Jesus.'

'A quarter of my salary.'

Another Jesus escapes me.

He's on $8,000 a month here. And I did most of the work. It's a bloody cruel world.

He answered my facial response, saying, 'Every time I get in a helicopter I receive three days towards my pension—qualifying yes. Qualifying days.'

'Really. Why?'

He lifts his shoulders, 'It's dangerous this country, yes, no?'

'It can be. Of course …'

'And each six months I spend in Lebanon is counted as one year towards, towards is right word, yes, to my pension?'

Talk about being made to feel Third World. These guys were getting paid sums that made a mockery of my salary, and we were both doing the same job. Already not in the best of form, my mood was darkening further.

'Jesus, you deserve all that and more for being French.'

He smiled and said, 'It is good pay and conditions, yes.'

I said, not in a bad way, 'Ah Yves, fuck off, will you, like a good man?'

His smile widened and I found it infectious. We sank beers and a couple more after these and then he quit because he was driving and I went one more.

When he came to our table I thanked the CO for the meal and said that he looked better with a fringe in front of his eyes.

He was not amused.

CHAPTER 18

Yves and Ness invited me along to Baalbek on Sunday. Ness wore his designer shades, which suited his shaved head. Though I didn't fancy the traffic jam, the ceaseless honking of car horns, I thought of the day yawning away in the house, in contrast to the chance to see the country I was spending so much time in, and said, 'Yes, sure, thanks, what time are we leaving?'

I liked to see as much as possible of Lebanon and Israel. I was naturally curious, inquisitive, and I was acutely aware that the occasion to sight-see presented itself on rare occasions. This was an opportunity for me to explore, to run my eye over part of Lebanon that I had not seen but knew of from reading history books.

'In half an hour, maybe,' Yves said.

'Fuck, yes,' Ness said, 'the quicker the better.'

Leaving the outskirts of Beirut we passed the Chateau Hotel Bernini and began an hour's journey, climbing into the Lebanese hills, passing through the fertile plain of the Bekaa valley, home of the poppy, of hash, the blow your mind out big-time drug farm. Baalbek is Hezbollah land, home to the Party of God. Its main street hosted a bronze statue but my eyes ricocheted off this to gaze at the acres upon acres of sun burned Roman ruins, set against the back drop of the snowy ridges of the Chouf Mountains. The scene snatched at my breath.

Baalbek is 86 kms from Beirut and until the mid 1990s was a no-go area for tourists. Hezbollah had radical anti-western doctrines and was associated with hostage taking. 10 metre high posters of Ayatollah Khomeini reminded me of their presence. Still, times had moved on. The dress code for visitors had relaxed a little, and it was possible to buy a beer in one of the town's small hotels. Staggering progress, really, when I considered Tyre in 1985 and the Amal's blanket ban on the sale of alcohol.

Baalbek, 'Sun City,' once enjoyed a reputation as one of the wonders of the world and mystics believe that special powers are attached to the courtyard complex. The site was originally Phoenician and dedicated to the god, Baal. It is suspected that human sacrifice occurred here and the temples a centre for all manner of sexual and licentious forms of worship. That is, according to the ancient tablets of *Ugarit*.

To reach the entrance we had to run the usual gauntlet of souvenir peddlers and offers of camel rides. The admission fee was 2,000 Lebanese pounds for natives and 4,000 for foreigners. A little over a dollar in the difference, and because the price was not much to begin with, none of us was into querying the anomaly.

The ruins are splendid examples of the rich culture enjoyed by the Romans. My mind boggled at the architectural world that existed over 2,000 years ago. Huge columns, marble and granite, ornate sarcophagi, large scale temples … The Six Columns of Jupiter majestic. Of course, labour in those days would not have presented a problem as there was an available and constant source of slaves, pay and insurance pay outs non-existent, no such thing as minimum wage, health and safety?

You worked till you dropped. Sounds like the fantasy world of some unscrupulous employers. Sounds to me like a sect had made its way to Ireland. Streams of tourists: boy scouts in wine coloured shirts, chador clad women with veiled faces, their husbands in cool white, walking a respectful distance in front of their wives—or should it read that the women were keeping their distance from their men, shepherding them? Groups of Italians and Germans armed with cameras and camcorders. Yves and Ness snapping goodo. Ness muttered, 'Oh, shit,' several times as he marvelled at the scene, once saying it out loud when he realised he'd run out of film. Apologising to the white suited men and their black clothed wives as they passed him, doing their damn best to ignore him. Here and there freshly watered flowerbeds scented the dry air.

We departed Baalbek at about 1pm, driving toward the mountains on a road impassable during the winter months. Along the way we passed Bedouin tents, walls bending in with the stiff breeze, ropes swaying like skipping ropes gone crazy. These were the last of the nomads?

I sat in the back, Yves driving. He thought the same about Ness's driving as I did. Ness was an excellent driver and hugely confident in his own ability, a scary sort of confidence. He carried a knife with him on patrol duties, explaining that it was to cut seat belts and free drivers and passengers from a car involved in an accident. A lesson he had learned the hard way, he said, allowing his silence to elaborate.

We climbed the mountain road, and soon far behind and

beneath us were Baalbek and the Bekaa valley. A car coming our way squeezed us to the verge. Sheer drop. I closed my eyes. Heights. Always bloody heights. This was turning out to be worse than the heli ride. We passed each other and Yves moved further in-road to the mountain flank.

Ness says, 'Fuck, Yves, you closed your eyes.'

'No. Never.'

'Yes, yes ...' Ness looks over his shoulder at me, 'he closed his eyes back there. Shee-it.'

Yves said, 'Okay, okay, I closed one eye. The one nearest you ...'

The art of compromise.

Dun coloured slopes carried grass like designer stubble. Farther along the way ice and snow and swatches of wild purple flowers. An old man in T-shirt and shorts skied down a long stretch of snow; the sun blazing behind him, the contrast striking. Down from the mountain, on a straight road, a green hand-glider moved across the valley like a lost and lonely soul searching for light.

A shack with smoke spiralling from a rusted chimney top attracted Yves into parking in front of it. A middle-aged woman said she wasn't in the café or restaurant business but would make us something to eat. Beef sandwiches with the fat dripping over the side of the bread, bottles of *Miranda* orange to wash them down, warm on the tongue and inhospitable to the belly. After moving on, Ness sucked his teeth to clear them of beef strings, and Yves picked at his with his small finger—habits that strummed my nerves.

We visited the Cedars, a grove containing some trees that are over 1,000 years old. Their trunks have a massive girth and their height can reach 30m. A disease found in a couple of the trees caused a major scare that the last remaining ancient cedars would be lost to a country once covered in vast forests of them. *Cedrus Libani* ... Tourist shops sold carvings made from the natural wastage of the cedar tree. Most of the trees are about 200 years old, of the more ancient variety; in 1550 there were 28 trees over a 1,000 years old; in 1660, 22; and in 1696, only 16. Today; 12. Naturally, it is against the law to cut down the trees, which are known to the locals as *arz ar-rab,* meaning *God's cedars.* Occasionally, access to the grove is curtailed, especially after heavy rain or when the snow is melting, so the roots won't be damaged by people walking on them when the ground is soft. Next up was Bcharre, the birthplace and final resting place of the great philosopher, Kahlil Gibran, author of *The Prophet.* Bcharre is a red-roofed town, picturesque and quaint and proud of its most famous son. Not far from the town centre is the Gibran museum, containing much of Gibran's paintings and drawings as well as his personal effects. In this area, I set the scene for the denouement of my Impac nominated novel, *The Broken Cedar.*

It was late by the time we returned to UNIFIL House, stuffed in a traffic jam for over an hour after we'd come down from the mountains. Ness would often punctuate the silence by saying, 'Fucking marvellous. '

Marvellous at the day's outings, the sights we'd seen. Marvellous in a different tone, meaning he was less than enamoured at Yves not being able to lean on the pedal.

When we got home we discovered that Hamid had left soup in a pot for us. His soup...

Diary entry: An entry made by a Finnish MP in a logbook from 1988 reads, 'Goodbye to Beirut – goodbye to Hamid's soup.' Eight years on he should know it hadn't improved.

***

Robert Fisk, the journalist, called into the house early one morning. He was hitching a ride to Naqoura with Italair. Yves was driving to the helipad and I was taking the other cruiser as we both had different places to go after we'd seen the flight off. *Pity the Nation* is a world best seller for Robert Fisk, and furnishes the reader with truthful insights rarely aspired to or managed by other war correspondents. The title of Robert's book was gleaned from Kahlil Gibran's book, *The Garden of the Prophet*. Robert casually dressed, carried a shoulder satchel, shook my hand and asked for a lift to the helipad.

'No problem. You can come with me or Yves. He might get you there quicker.'

'No, I'll go with you.'

Robert talked a lot—Algeria was the hellhole of the Middle East at that time, with daily news reports of fanatics committing dreadful atrocities against foreigners and the inhabitants of remote villages. He was on his way to interview the PLO 'prisoner' in MP Coy, to focus attention on his plight.

He mentioned an Irish officer's name to me, '… do you know him?'

I did and I didn't and so said, 'Does he talk a lot?'

'Yes,' he smiled, 'he does.'

'Yeah, I know him.'

He smiled and looked to the side window, fell silent.

Did he think I was hinting at him to quieten?

Maybe. Or perhaps he was thinking about how'd I'd strung a characteristic to a man in order to suss his name and was amused by this?

As we approached the helipad, driving through the gate manned by Lebanese Military Police, he said, 'Murt,' he said, 'never, ever, get up in a Lebanese huey. I hear from the Italians that they are very badly maintained.'

'Robert,' I said, 'never ever get too fond of travelling anywhere by helicopter.'

Not the most comforting thing to hear when you're about to board a chopper.

Five-years later Robert and I discussed my novel, *After Kafra*, and the main character; a UN soldier suffering from Post-Traumatic Stress Disorder. His comments—that the incident at the centre of the story was not enough to cause PTSD—as a hard-bitten journalist used to seeing war and death, were fair comment. However, I still contend that the incident portrayed was enough to cause the disorder—people react differently to traumatic events. The majority of people deal with things and move on in their lives, while others are damaged and remain damaged unless they receive help for the condition. Anyone can come across the scene of say, a traffic accident, and witness a teenager's decapitated head on the road—a year later, perhaps two … the disorder could darken their every living moment. Research among UK soldiers discovered a strain of PTSD associated with peacekeeping duties as opposed to peace enforcement, primarily triggered by the peacekeeper's feeling of powerlessness and helplessness in a time of conflict. Emasculated soldiers. I lived in the shoes of the main character who was in fact part-Norwegian, part Fijian and part Irish and built it round the incident in Kafra, driven by 'What if …' What if my mind hadn't left Kafra behind? Would I have become a hardened and determined boozer, numbing my hurt, wrecking my family's head? What would I have done? What support mechanism was there for me? This was a book that touched the raw nerve of a lot of soldiers because they saw themselves in it. It was grass roots realism.

The book was real and though I was not the character of *Harry Kyle*, per se, I wore his shoes and the book had an authentic setting, death, destruction, and moreover an honesty that bruised and asked searching questions of the reader. What did the army do about its lame dogs?

Certainly the topic of war damaged soldiers will never be out of vogue. I often think about the children in war zones—no doubt their lives are ruined and they must suffer awful from PTSD, and yet what help is there for them? None at all. Living in a war zone is all about the basics—surviving.

CHAPTER 19

Terese disliked seeing me at a desk when she was cleaning the offices. Normally, she'd look at me from under her eyebrows and carry on hoovering or dusting, spraying furniture polish, lips silently protesting my presence. I'd seen her talking to the fat woman who'd I'd bounced about in the Caprice and if looks could kill I'd have been shredded. She blanked me one morning, not even a look from under her eyebrows. The poison in her ear had a lasting effect.

I liked to write for an hour in the mornings before the house wakened and the day lost the run of itself. Not long into that routine my notebook computer crashed, which was a bitch because I was midway into a short story that was shaping up very well. Susan the secretary gave me a name and I drove to the far side of Beirut. Without much difficulty I found a little warehouse in the back street, behind a launderette and left the PC in for repair. It was fixable for $50 but there was no warranty—Pepe said it could last a day, a week, five years. I bought the risk. The notebook didn't fail me again.

I was due down the following day to Naqoura for the dogface conference. The pilot across from the MP desk, said, 'Murt, will I book your seat on the heliflight for tomorrow?'

'No, thanks.'

He arched his eyebrow and said, 'How will you get down?'

'I'll drive.'

How else did he think? It's 114 kms from Beirut to the Israeli border.

He shook his head, 'You save time by flying.'

'I don't like flying.'

He pursed those elastic lips and frowned, 'Crazy man. And you drive back up, too, yes?'

'No, I'll stay overnight.'

'Still, four hours unnecessary driving,' he held up the right amount of fingers.

'Listen, Franco, sorry, it's not the pilots, it's the choppers.'

He shrugged with exasperation and touched his heavy gold neck chain; 'Mama mia ...'

***

The following morning I got my pistol from the safe, the keys and logbook of UNIFIL 1775 off the desk, and headed off just as the party lights were dying on the luxury cruiser in the bay. The pistol of the Irish army at that time was the Browning Automatic, which was a misnomer because the pistol wasn't automatic, but could be if you were to file down the sear. We called the pistol 'The Bap'. 1958 pattern web-belt and holster, faded green. Firing a pistol for the first time, well afterwards you never look at a western movie with the same eye.

Five yards from a figure 2 target, a man's head and torso, and after loosening three rounds you find upon inspecting the target that you're wide of the bull, chipping the wings. I never fired a weapon in anger … five trips to Lebanon and the only time I cocked a weapon was on range practice and in a UNIFIL pistol shooting competition, finishing mid-table in the league.

I left early; BT; Before Terese, and hit Sidon about an hour later, driving south. Pulling into a café at the fish market, I drank an espresso and enjoyed a croissant, looking at my unattended vehicle through the P in Phoenicia, my pistol under the driving seat, alien to my teaching and beliefs, but the way I saw it was this: you can have all the guns you want hanging out of you, but if someone gets the drop on you, you're cooked. You may simply unbuckle your holster and go along with what happens. What else can you do? Politely decline? I'd always wanted to visit the crusader sea castle and never had the chance. Fellas I'd have been with were either in too much of hurry to stop or had no interest in viewing the ruins.

It was natural for me to visit places of heritage. In Kildare I was brought up under the eye of a Viking age round tower, within walking distance of the ruins of Blackfriar Abbey and a Franciscan monastery where the earls of Kildare were laid to rest. I've visited Clonmacnoise, Grange stone circle, Tara, on many occasions—these places are gifts from the past to the soul of our nation and therefore worthy of care and respect. And here I was, in the archaeological hot pot of the world; a smorgasbord of delights. When I was in class in the vocational school in Kildare, a visiting priest asked each of us our career choice. When I said I was interested in archaeology he gave me a long steady look. He thought I was taking the mickey, but I was dead serious. He'd been hearing down the rows: 'Carpenter, Father;

soldier, Father; mechanic, Father,' and so on. Mostly trades, as I suppose you would expect to hear in a vocational school. I'd thrown him, I suppose.

Now, the opportunity to slake my desire had arrived. The sea castle, *Qasr al-Bahr*, dates from the 12th century and is reached by a causeway. The crusaders built the castle as a defence against sea and land raiders. It was originally the site of a Phoenician temple to the god, Melkart. The rooms were vast and dark; old rusting cannonballs strewn about. Each floor is connected by a winding staircase that leads to the roof which affords a terrific view of the old city and fishing harbour. For a few moments I pictured in my head the way the castle looked in its heyday, exercising my imagination. I remembered a cover of the Litani UNIFIL magazine; one of Tibnin castle and UN soldiers walking along a grassy slope, mentioning 'New Crusaders ...' Obviously, the editor didn't know his history for the Arabs saw crusaders as barbarians and indeed contemporary Arabic reports show how backward the crusader was in terms of medical practice, hygiene, and respect for prisoners of war—they were brutal.

I felt honoured to be here amidst so much history, a history I would never have gotten to see, or know, had I stayed back in Ireland, counting down the days to my retirement. It was a privilege to be in such a place. But there was always a constant reminder that I was here for a reason, and this always intruded on my thoughts and appreciation towards this ancient land. Out of the corner of my eye I saw that my cruiser was beginning to attract the attention of local youths and I decided to get a move on.

When I hit the Litani Bridge I pulled over and brought my

web-belt and its holster from under the driver's seat and fitted them around my waist, attached the clip on my red lanyard to its counterpart on the pistol grip. Technically, I was in the area of operations and had to be armed. I was also supposed to have someone with me, or be part of at least a two-car team; a problem I didn't think of until I was well along the coastal road and approaching the last Fijian checkpoint before Charlie Swing-gate. I met in with some other UN vehicles and tail-gated them through the SLA checkpoint.

I attended the dogface meeting, listening to the briefings, giving my own in the tired old format used by dogfaces and section heads: 'Traffic accidents two, theft of UN property one, escorts five, helipad duties 18 ...'

There was a barbecue that night in Camp Tara, so I spent the night in MP Coy. Comdt Carbury, the army press officer, was in Tara and we had a pint together. He was accompanying a band that the army sent out to entertain the troops. It broke the monotony, I suppose. The troops, those I spoke to, would have preferred Christy Moore, or the Fureys. Then again, maybe Christy just didn't want the hassle.

Next morning, I showered and shaved and left MP Coy, and Naqoura camp, and parked up the road a little to await a UN car that might be going my way.

The next few days on my wind-down time in Beirut, I bought a few books in Antoine Libraire, and went to Bourj-Hammoud, the Armenian quarter, with Peter, as gold was cheaper there than anywhere else in Lebanon, or so he insisted. I'd made acquaintances with an elderly Armenian writer who managed a book shop quite close to the American University of Beirut, and said goodbye to him.

He'd given me much to ponder about the craft of writing. Before returning to Beirut I drove to Yardze, the Ministry of Defence building on the outskirts of the city, and asked a sergeant in the guardroom for permission to take photographs of the new *Monument of Peace*—ten-stories of military paraphernalia ensnared in layers of concrete and sandbags. This sculpture was designed by the French artist, Armand Fernandez. Its 5,000 ton structure contains real Soviet T-55 tanks, armoured vehicles and artillery. The sergeant rang his superiors and emerged a few minutes later to say, 'Yes, okay, but I take the photos.' I agreed. Photographing and sketching any military installation in any part of the world is frowned upon, which was why I had sought permission in the first place. Problems can arise when you are photographing an area you don't realise is a military installation—no ostensible evidence suggests that it is—because it belongs to a terrorist organisation.

One curious aspect of my time in Beirut was this: after the *Grapes of Wrath* there were high-level talks held in Naqoura between the Israelis, Lebanese, Syrians, French ... top diplomats trying to prevent a return to the nadir of the spring months; but everything was discussed—even who went to Naqoura on the first helicopter. The Syrians wanted to know why the Americans went ahead of them ... they were told they could have the first chopper out of Naqoura. This sort of nit-picking went on; an indication of how suspicious the Syrians are of the west and vice-versa. I think the point to bear in mind is this—all of the trouble in the Middle East is essentially caused by the existence of Israel. The three countries in the region most determined to see the obliteration of Israel are Iran, Syria and to a lesser degree for obvious reasons, Iraq. Until Israel is accepted by Iran and Syria as a nation with sovereign rights, there will never be peace in the Middle East. So the carousel runs like this—conflict; horrible wastage of civilian life and destruction of property; talks about holding talks; breakdown in the talks about having talks; talks; a cease-fire, breakdown, more talks, truce, lick the wounds and prepare for a further campaign ...conflict ...

One small example of how all this impacts on the ordinary civilian who simply wants to live a peaceful life is this: Rida told me about a fella who was a Christian and was being conscripted to join the Lebanese Army. After his training he would be posted south. The idea being to confront the mainly Christian SLA with Lebanese Army Christians. He went to a specialist who for $1,000 put him sitting in the waiting room, handed him a piece of gum and told him to chew on it. Later, he took the chewing gum from his patient, stretched it to a thin thread, and lay it along the patient's leg, x- rayed it in situ. Result: the guy failed his army medical – he'd sweated for weeks, worrying if the Lebanese recruiting officer would send him for a second x-ray. If this man had gone south he would have been a frontline troop in the war against Israel and their proxy ally ... he did not want to soldier, did not want to fight, and $1,000 was a lot of money, perhaps five or six months salary, money he needed to care for his family. And that's small scale stuff compared to what else happens, for instance, the lowering of dead children into mass graves.

★★★

Back within the fold at MP Coy, I was working in Traffic Section, under a Norwegian lieutenant who operated a zero tolerance policy when it came to traffic offences. Then I was slotted into the Special Investigation Section, and sent all over the AO on random drug searches with the sniffer dogs and on rotation searches, too. Lots of them.

Smuggling was rife. A couple of Polish guys were caught bringing prohibited items across the border and the following day were sent home in disgrace. Again the soldiers were searched. They'd taped packets of cigarettes to their bodies. Another scam discovered was this one: remove an old car radio from a UN vehicle and install a new one in its stead, unwired. In Israel the piece was removed and sold, and the process repeated.

In the war zone that was Lebanon, the pattern of smuggling varied in accordance to whatever was happening on the political landscape. When the north of the country was in turmoil there was money to be made by smuggling goods into the UNIFIL controlled area and Israel. When the north of the country picked itself up, formed a government, re-introduced taxes, the role was reversed. Always, though, no matter the shift of balance in Lebanon, Israel was a smuggler's milk and honey. Often, while wearing civvie attire, I'd be approached by people, usually old guys along HaGa'aton Boulevard in Nahariya, and asked if I'd brought over whiskey or cigarettes. I valued my career too much to take the risk, but I was tempted at times, sorely so, to give it a swing. Make no mistake about it, I wanted to, and if you asked me if it were through an innate honesty that I didn't succumb, I would say, 'Yes, that, and fear of the consequences if caught. A combination of the two.'

You can be the most upright soul born but plinths aren't made for human feet—the clay won't set—and besides, pedestals are made for falling off.

I visited Muhammad, Ali's son, a lot. He had a clothes shop near his dad's. Ali's shop was closed more often that it was open; he had problems with his health and trade wasn't as strong as it had been in years gone by.

Muhammad had curly dark hair and was about 25. He was friendly, talkative, slightly nervous, as though at any moment he expected to hear bad news. He had large, expressive brown eyes. He always offered a beer and liked to chat. Never in a hurry to push me out of the door. Me. Who spent more time looking than buying. His shop, his home, was of corrugated iron and steel girders and bulky wooden crossbeams. He said, 'I like people come into my shop smiling, not frowning.'

'I'm having a bad day.'

'Not you, my friend, not you, but some come in here and they are so sad they make me almost cry.'

He went on to say he disliked the Swedes, '… toffee-nosed, always they pick up my clothes like they were dirty rags. I charge them $40 for say a pair of jeans and I charge you $20. See. The Ghana man and Nepalese come in and never buy. Never. The Fiji, he clifty (steal) the shop if he could.'

He spoke of the Lebanese army getting, 'A big eye,' that they'd caught a man who'd forged banknotes and gave him 20 years in prison. And of dancing with, 'The General's wife,' when he was nine years old at a party in the camp. He was full of talk.

For the weekend I'd put in a transport request to Playtime. I wanted to visit Jerusalem and stay overnight. Duty commitments

roped up those who'd expressed an interest in travelling and so
I went on my own. I booked into a hotel, had something to eat,
entering the city by the Lion's gate and walked the streets of the
Old City. The streets were empty, traders had rolled down their
blinds and gone home. Lanterns on steel archways bridging the
tiny street came on, some remained blind. Entering the Church
of the Holy Sepulchre, I glanced at the crosses notched into the
columns by the crusaders. The church is vast, has vaulted high
ceilings, smells of burning candle and incense, and resembles a
building site; either a work-in-progress or something started but
halted because of upheld planning objections. Pigeons flew here
and there, cooing. I paid my respects and lit candles for friends
and family, and those gone ahead. Wherever ahead is.

'Jesus Christ died here, give a dollar,' says one holy man.

I didn't. Chuggers on the street was acceptable but not inside
one of the most revered places in Christendom.

A week or so before the first homebound rotations were to
begin, I was sent along with a Norwegian MP to oversee and
assist the Irish MPs from Gallows Green in searching luggage.

This NCO presented himself at my table and opened his
suitcase, full of cigarette cartons. I looked at him and said, 'What
are you playing at?'

Then someone approached me and said, 'Murt, leave him,
he's not breaking any law. He might declare them at customs.'

'And if he doesn't, then what? We'll have aided and abetted
him.'

'Murt ...'

'Don't Murt me. How many packets of cigarettes have they
been told that they're allowed to bring home?'

He didn't answer. Two or three cartons. I'd have let four, five go by. But not a caseload. And there was more than that. The soldier had another case.

'What's in it?'

'I don't have the key. I'm bringing it home for someone else.'

'Your number, rank and name are on it.'

'I don't have the key.'

'When you do, call me. I'll be in MP Coy, with your case.'

If soldiers were brazen enough to pull this stunt in front of the MPs, you had to wonder what the fuck they were getting up to behind our backs. The MP didn't primarily worry too much about cigarettes or booze being smuggled home—it was weapons and drugs that caused us concern. It was possible to buy a pistol, break down its parts, and bring it home. Has this happened? I don't know. No one can say for certain, but it was possible.

★★★

It was almost over. My fifth trip abroad. Epeli held a small kava party in the MP club, a traditional Fijian farewell do … again the kava, the acquirement of the 1,000 yard stare. The goodbyes for good this time. It was Epeli's final trip abroad and mine too, or so I'd thought, forgetting that I'd thought the same on four other occasions.

Take-off at Beirut was delayed by the mini-tornadoes out to sea, visible through the oval window, more than one, nature's spinning tops. Were they heading inland? It didn't appear so but the pilot wasn't taking any chances. When they blew off elsewhere, the airbus started for the runway and then jerked to a sudden stop. Ground staff on a baggage cart had almost collided with the plane.

The pilot, non-plussed, said, '… they're only getting used to having airplanes moving about on the runway.'

It was a crazy country in a crazy time, and I was glad to be returning home once more.

CHAPTER 20

During my stay at home, after that tour, I was becoming increasingly frustrated and troubled by the ringing noise in my left ear. The flight home had been a painful experience and I thought at one point my eardrum was about to burst. This hadn't happened before or since. Was it just a freak flight? In the months preceding my trip to Lebanon I'd seen four doctors about the complaint and their reactions were similar. They didn't want to know, really; said there was nothing that could be done for the condition. No cure. One examined my ear for a sign of infection, the others didn't. Sleeping pills were prescribed, which I used once or twice, but a lack of sleep wasn't the issue as I had developed a routine to ensure that I slept, though there were nights I lost the battle. The noise itself was the problem. I was looked at by the doctors as a chancer, as someone who was climbing aboard the gravy train that travelled to the High Court and returned with carriages filled to the brim with taxpayers' money. Were they right?

Was I?

A chancer?

Certainly. I had tinnitus and if people were receiving compensation for the condition, then yeah, I was going to take my chance. That was the problem: when soldiers began to win their tinnitus and hearing cases in court, doctors were inundated with patients who had hitherto been quiet about their hearing condition. Many soldiers were unaware that they could sue the army for negligence regarding their loss of hearing and for tinnitus. When they found out, well ... the floodgates opened. What else should they have done? Leave the money alone? If there was no culpability on the part of the authorities then why did the claimants win so many cases in court and on the steps of the court? What are the origins of these court cases? Was it because the army medical authorities sometimes tried to discharge someone because of his poor hearing, or in the posters that appeared frequently on unit notice boards about this soldier, that man, suffering from a medical condition derived from his service in the PDF—the compensation culture, as with the general population, always existed in the army—the hearing issue just became a monster.

Another point: a soldier didn't simply say he had a hearing problem. He had to undergo tests for his hearing on a few occasions and attend ear consultants to prove it. Clichéd as it might read, it wasn't just about the money. I had a problem. I still have a problem. If you had to pick your problems then tinnitus, the Latin word for, 'To ring,' was one you'd choose ahead of many worse diseases and illnesses. What I suffer from is manageable. But let me tell you this: tinnitus in one ear is bad enough, but to have it in both must be altogether quite literally, maddening. A suicide prompt.

★★★

No cure. No empathy. No further medical investigation. I was disbelieved it seemed. Public and media opinion was mounting against the soldier. The cost was going to be prohibitive to the State, we were told. Soldiers were cast as villains—stagecoach bandits—it didn't worry me what people said or felt compelled to write. If I end up in Heaven with some of them I'll book a ticket to Hell. I rang a solicitor in Newbridge and made an appointment to speak with him about the possibility of taking litigation against the Minister of Defence for damage caused to my left ear. I was sent to an audiologist in Dublin who measured my head, looked into my ears, and then put me in a soundproof room, fitted headphones to my ears and alternatively fed a variety of noises to both ears, testing for hearing loss and tinnitus. The hearing loss was minimal, but a dip inside my left ear indicated the presence of tinnitus and the noise I had picked out was identical to that selected by a vast majority of tinnitus sufferers; a high-pitched din.

'Well, you were right about your hearing,' she said, 'there's no discernible loss.'

'The tinnitus ...'

'People tell me they'd sooner be deaf and hear nothing than have to listen to that.'

On the basis of the audiologist's report, the solicitor took my case. He had dealt with other similar cases, as he practiced in Newbridge, which was an army town. There had been a lack of training regarding the dangers of being exposed to noise, and years of cutbacks within the army, running it on a shoestring budget, perhaps knowing that hearing protection was advisable and necessary, well, those budgetary decisions caught up with the very people who'd kept the army in the dark ages.

There was also a growing awareness by the soldier of his rights. A revolution was taking place. Its origins sourced to the late 1980s when soldiers' low pay was increased when there were fears of mutiny occurring within the ranks. How real or imagined this fear was is difficult to gauge. There were certainly rumblings and much discontent. Soldiers' wives set up an organisation to say the things their husbands could not, and this in turn, to diffuse the situation, carved the way forward for the birth of PDFORRA, Permanent Defence Forces Other Ranks Representative Association.

For the first time soldiers were given the right to speak openly about their welfare, pay and conditions. In reality, the association had no teeth and lacked a groundswell support base. Many soldiers, those who want to develop their military careers and young soldiers, do not want to be seen as rocking the boat, being a shit-stirrer, and keep their heads low. But PDFORRA was not allowed to represent their members on overseas duty. And the consultative status of the organisation is akin to winning a free ticket to the sheik's harem and reading, 'as a eunuch,' in small print.

★★★

Shortly after I returned home, I was approached and asked if I'd like to travel to Naqoura as an MP sergeant. I wasn't home a year. People were not volunteering for Lebanon anymore. It was no longer a sought after mission. Leb weariness, perhaps?

Cutbacks in unit strength? I said I needed time to think about it, which wasn't the thing to say at all. Not in light of what my wife had said the last time—she was Leb sick. But I hated the mundane barrack life, the regularity of 24 hour duties, clocking in at least two a week, which meant 48 hours in work, adding another 8 for a day duty and you'd put in a minimum of 56 hours in a working week. More often than not, the Military Policeman in the provost section would do three 24 hour duties in a week. When it came to totting up the hours worked, the authorities didn't tot up the man's rest time after his completion of a 24 out of bed duty. In the end I think 4 hours was agreed upon, thus pushing up the MP's sum of hours worked. I couldn't understand why more fellas didn't jump at the chance to seize an overseas trip and leave all that palaver behind. I think part of the problem lay in the fact that soldiers' partners, with the upswing in the economy and increased job availability, were joining the workforce and the soldier was obviously required to spend more time at home, money not being a driving factor that entailed his having to travel abroad any more.

There were other issues at that time: the army had an attack of ageism. The army was gearing itself towards the younger generation. Okay, granted, the older troops were no longer fit enough to jump out of helicopters or abseil, but there were a lot of men who had given a lot of service home and abroad to their country and this was forgotten in the rush to check the dates on their birth certs. There was also another small factor in my decision to travel: In 1985 when I asked to serve overseas I was given a tour of duty—a part of me felt I owed a favour.

***

I walked home across the plains. It was late and the moon was full of itself. Sheep stirred and I heard voices from a furze draped knoll, young guys popping cans and smoking hash, the stink of it alive in the dead air.

'Fuck off, give us that, that's mine.'

'You're a bad bastard.'

'Get your hands off my tinnie, fucker ya.'

The screech of a girl ... laughter.

Products of broken homes, alcoholic parents, abused, no self-esteem, no self-respect, and none for others, either. This was their life. My shadow long on the magnesium grass, footstep light, so as not to alert the party to my presence. Jesus, if I keep going abroad, am I opening a door to my kids and allowing them access to that sort of life? Sitting in the furze, in sheep shite? How can you keep an eye on them from 4,000 miles? The mother is the fulcrum of a healthy relationship, of keeping kids on a level footing. If she isn't functioning properly, at 100 per cent ... the kids end up in shite. Then again, there are many kids like that whose father's never went abroad.

I entered the kitchen, went to the range and stood with my back to the chrome rail. There was a smell of freshly cooked apple tart in the oven. Bernadette walked in from the hall, after putting Barry to bed.

'You're late,' Bernadette said, checking the wall clock to confirm how late.

'Yeah, I was finishing off a report.'

'Barry's looking for you ...'

'I'll go up to him in a sec. Where's Colin?'

'He's on the green with the lads, playing soccer.'

'I was asked to go overseas.'

Silence, giving way to the kettle on the sizzle.

'Do you want to go?'

'I don't know. What do you think?'

'Is there no one else they can ask?'

I supposed that there was. Definitely. I shrugged and said, 'They asked me.'

'Do you think it'll stand to you when it comes to promotion?' Naively, and naïve to think it, I said, 'It could. I don't know about that, not anymore.'

'If you're home for Christmas, then ... once you're home for Christmas.'

Walking into work the next morning, the Curragh biting hard at the back of my ears, racehorses clip-clopping across the road en route to the all-weather gallops, a friend of mine, Willie, pulled over in his car, wound down his window and said something about John Lynch. Passing traffic drowned his words. Willie was a medic and a PDFORRA representative. John had made the TV and newspapers recently, after he and some Italian colleagues had been taken prisoner by the Hezbollah. The UN personnel were reported as having being roughed up by their captors. John returned home for a brief holiday after his ordeal and then went back to Lebanon.

I crossed the road to speak with Willie. I was instructing in the MP School at the time and had classes on that day. Racing against the clock as usual. 'Willie,' I said ... My words trailed off. Willie had bad news in his face.

'John Lynch was killed in a helicopter crash last night.'

'God, that's terrible ...'

'Five killed,' Willie said, 'four Italians.'

I walked up the hill into work, noted the flag at half-mast on the Water Tower, in my head praying for John and his family. I never read the full report into the circumstances surrounding the awful tragedy. The helicopter was on a night-time training exercise, was last seen climbing from a UNIFIL post, high into the darkness, and then dropped from the sky, into a wadi. In Lebanon two Italian MPs, walking towards MP Coy, had been invited along for the flight. One gladly accepted the offer, the other reluctantly declined, having had a prior commitment. Listening to him retell the story in the duty room at MP Coy I dwelt upon the vagaries of fate.

15 Oct: *Diary entry*: Spend a lot of time thinking about John this evening. Say a prayer for him. I think of other friends who've passed on down the years: Richard Cusack, a kid who lived some doors from me in Lourdesville, and Albert Kindregan with whom I used to run and pal around. You wonder and you pray ... and you deal with the hurt because you have to ... My shaving gear and towel, a few books, a notebook and pens on the table, a wallet, the green handgrip with the tricolour flash in the corner—ready for the morning departure to McKee Barracks, the form-up point for the chalk prior to travelling to the airport. When am I going to end this? Why don't I? I must love it —the pain of leaving, the joy of coming home, the in-between part. Every trip is different. I must love it.

***

Among those travelling out with me were Phil O'Neill, John Jeffers and Mick Fitzmaurice. Phil was CSM in 1996, and we'd known each other from quite a while back. There was no problem with my leave application – it would be my first time to travel home on leave from an overseas mission.

The CO of MP Coy was Comdt Gleeson, whose brother was killed in the Niemba massacre in the Congo. He was on a year long tour of duty and about to commence his second six-month period. Someone came into the traffic section office and told me that the CO wanted to have a talk. I went over and knocked on his door, saluted and waited.

He looked at me, 'Can I help you?'

'The CSM said you wanted to see me.'

'No. I'll see you in the briefing room with the others.'

'Oh, my apologies, Sir.'

All we heard in the briefing room was what he expected of us. When he was done and gone we looked at each other. We certainly knew we were back on the job.

Nothing much in MP Coy had changed. Khamis the prisoner had been allowed into Jordan, passing through Israel in manacles. His old cells became the dumping ground for thousands of MP reports, investigations into all manners of incidents. An attempt was made to hand over to me an ongoing investigation into allegations of sexual impropriety by a soldier toward Lebanese children. But as I was involved in traffic section I side-stepped the case and left it to someone else to deal with when they came out on Chalk II.

The officer in charge of Traffic was Finnish, Hekka, then

there was Roy Mortensen; Norway; Leszek Sokolowski; Poland; Monoku; Fiji, Timo; Finnish.

Hekka, like most Scandinavians with whom I'd worked, operated a zero tolerance policy. Roy was missing a little finger, had a twitch in his eye, and had lost a national boxing final on points in Norway, the winner going to the Olympics. Leszek's son played junior international table tennis for Poland. My partner for most traffic check duty excursions in Lebanon and Israel was Leszek.

One morning a young woman arrived into the office. I was alone, working at the computer. She had tears in her eyes and flagged a report at me, saying, 'This is not true.'

'What isn't?'

She handed me the report and I leafed through it. Run of the mill. She was deemed responsible for causing a minor traffic accident. Hekka had investigated the case.

'I am not at fault,' she said.

I sat her down and went through the accident with her. She showed me a scrap of paper bearing the registration number of a UNIFIL vehicle. She said the driver and his passenger had witnessed the accident.

'This is new information. How did you come by it?' I said.

'They buy in my brother's shop and when he told them about the accident they said, no, no … they were there. We saw what happened. They are Polish.'

'Leave it with me.'

When she was gone I went through our list of UNIFIL vehicles and their location. The vehicle was attached to the Polish Engineers Company—Polengcoy, in Jwayya.

Hekka, when he reported in, shook his head and said in his modulated voice, 'Maybe this was arranged for them to say this?'

I caught his drift.

'Perhaps. Leszek should speak with them and see if that's so.'

According to Leszek, who obtained statements in Polish from the witnesses, which I helped him translate, the soldiers were sincere. He'd verified that they were present at the location and parked at a spot opposite the gates of the transport yard at roughly the time the accident occurred. Hekka rang the transport officer and arranged to interview him. It turned out that if the officer had been held accountable for causing a traffic accident it would have had a detrimental consequence on his bonus from the UN ... so he set in train a little scheme to ensure he qualified for his extra money. He blew a gasket in the office. He did not understand why the case had been re-opened, couldn't get his head around the idea. He had what you call a closed mind.

Sometimes things went awry. Monoku had to return home for a domestic reason, and I was to take over a case in which a young Israeli soldier had been badly injured by a UN vehicle when crossing the road at a junction outside Haifa. Monoku had already been to the scene of the accident as the investigating MP and as I was now dealing with the case I wanted to see the accident location for myself. He brought me there, and I took a sketch, went into the nearby army barracks and spoke with an Israeli officer about the latest medical information concerning the soldier. I put all this in my report and photos and sketch of the scene. Two-weeks after submission, Monoku gone to Fiji, the UN field service driver called in. Irate. He said the location stated in the report wasn't where the accident had occurred, it was at a crossing further back, '… and the soldier didn't cross at the junction, he came out of some bushes at the side of the road.' All I could do was take more statements. The truth was in there somewhere.

Routine in Traffic Section. We checked the speed gun to ensure it was reading properly and headed off to carry out speed and documentation checks in the Area of Operations, sometimes dropping in to a different unit to interview a driver or a witness to an accident. Once a week Leszek and I crossed the border to carry out speed checks in Israel. A couple of mornings I stopped Timur Goksel, the United Nations spokesperson, in South Lebanon. He'd smile as I recorded his details, and then drive away. Afterwards, if the road was quiet of UN traffic, we'd go into Nahariya and drink café lattes under the awning of the Penguin Café, chill in the early morning sun, and people watch.

Speed checks in Lebanon were a different proposition entirely. Not that we didn't have our coffee breaks, we did, but often we were stuck north of the border when Charlie Swing-gate was closed because of fears that an attack was imminent by terrorists, freedom fighters, whatever, and now and then we got grief from UN drivers. For example: on the coastal road in a village that had a one-sided street of homes and garages and shops, we set up a speed trap. The speed limit was 30 km per hour in a built-up area. Leszek manned the speed gun, radar equipment with red neon digits. A UNIFIL cruiser came into view, its blue and white UN flag stiff in the breeze, weather worn. I knew it was travelling above the regulation speed and looking back up the road at Leszek, about 50 metres away, he confirmed this with a wave. I waved the vehicle down and approached the driver. A Ghanaian captain, his passenger a private.

I saluted him. He was angry. The whites of his eyes had red in them.

He said, 'What's the problem?'

'You were speeding.'

'I was not. How am I speeding? I was not speeding.'

'Well, let's see what the speed gun says.'

Leszek was walking towards us. Meanwhile I stopped another UN vehicle and checked the driver for his documentation, a cursory glance at it, because the Ghanaian captain was by now shouting the odds at Leszek.

I went over and said, 'What's wrong here?'

The speed reading flashed 47 kmh.

'This is not a built-up area, this is not a built-up area ...' he said, losing the run of himself.

Kids were playing with a ball, others watched us with increasing curiosity. I remembered Madjil Silm in '92 and the scene of a traffic accident that Mickey Rall and I had responded to, the throng of kids, the air thick with hostility, the glares of the adults from their homes ... their village bombed and the UN does nothing to prevent it happening.

'Calm down,' I said.

This made him worse.

'I am a captain. Who do you think you are? I will report you.'

'Show me your UN I.D. card and your driver's permit.'

Snorting and sighing he dug them out of his wallet and handed them to me. I recorded his details on the speed check proform and said, 'I think you are too angry to drive.'

I looked past him to the private and said, 'Have you a driver's permit?'

'No, Sir.'

He was trying to stop a smile from breaking out.

'Step out of the car, Sir, please.'

The officer's demeanour changed.

'Why?'

'It'll be easier for me to put on the handcuffs.'

Deadpan, drop-dead serious.

'You are arresting me?'

'I can't let you drive in a UN vehicle in a temper. It's as bad as driving with alcohol in your system.'

'I'm not angry,' he said, quietly.

'You're sure?'

The private turned his head away.

'Yes, very sure.'

'Please sign here to say that you were stopped at this location, and I'll give you a copy.'

It was killing him to remain quiet, the vein in his neck bulging.

***

Some of the cases dealt with: A Fijian soldier under the influence of kava fell asleep behind the wheel of his UNIFIL vehicle and veered into a front garden of a small house, killing an old man who'd been sleeping on a mat outdoors. A five-year old boy darted across the road in front of a UN vehicle and was literally scalped, badly injured. Speaking to the doctor in Tyre, Najib

Hospital, about his condition the doctor said he would make a full recovery and went on to speak about his medical career, how he'd visited Ireland, recalled an Irish short story he'd read entitled, *The Sniper*, in which a man unwittingly shoots his brother who is a member of the opposing army. It reminded him of what was going on in his country. Another incident involved the detonation of a roadside bomb on the McKenzie Road, in which four or five Fijian soldiers were fortunate to escape with their lives. The force of the bomb impacted on the bonnet, twisting the engine and metal skin into a grotesque sculpture. The make-up of the bomb contained no steel ball-bearings and I think it was designed to maim and not kill.

I was once again glad to be leaving this place; there didn't seem to be an end to this sort of thing. I had my ticket for home, flying MEA, Middle Eastern Airways, from Beirut, staying overnight in the Mayflower Hotel, catching an early flight to Heathrow the next morning. There was a fear of Charlie Swing-gate being closed – it was happening a lot. I think what saved it from coming under constant guerrilla bombardment was the fact it was a main crossing point for Lebanese civilians crossing in and out of, 'Free Lebanon.'

The nights were a different proposition, when the checkpoint was closed. Often you would hear the sound of rockets being fired and machine gun fire raking the air. Illumination shells would light up the skies, umbrellas of amber light lingered. In the mornings you heard either through the grapevine or at the Operations Brief, the events of the night before. Always, before travelling in UNIFIL's theatre of operations, we rang UNIFIL Operations to check if it was safe to travel the roads. There could be a blanket ban on travel or certain roads and areas might be off-limits, all this determined by the level of tension and conflict that might be prevalent. Insofar as it was possible then, the UN tried to keep its soldiers out of harm's way, but as with any war zone, there was no guarantee regarding anyone's safety. This type of lifestyle was accepted by UNIFIL. They had neither the firepower nor the manpower to try and effect a peace through force ... so it endured and did the best it could in the worst possible circumstances. It provided humanitarian aid, facilitated meetings between the concerned parties, bore witness to the atrocities perpetrated by both sides, buried the bodies of those of its soldiers who were caught in harm's way. It lived a lie; acted like a partner in a bad marriage who decided to stay for the sake of the kids. Maybe not a bad thing if there is peace in the home, but if there's not ...

CHAPTER 21

Before daybreak, MP Beirut drove us to the airport. About a 20 minute ride away. The streets dark and empty, hours before the city turned into the valley of honking horns and smog world. The MPs tried not to show it but I could tell they were pissed at having to rise at an ungodly hour to perform a task which they believed wasn't part of their job description—the ferrying of MP Coy CO and others from one side of Beirut to the other.

Early in the tour I'd heard Military Police moaning about doing this sort of task and was surprised by it, because helping each other out had been formerly a run of the mill thing for Military Police. Cribs confined to being used as a taxi service or the detachment as a B & B by members of different units. Many times I drove Military Police and other personnel to and from airports in Israel and Lebanon. Yes, there were times that I felt put upon, that certain favours asked of me went a step beyond the mark of what was reasonable to expect, but mostly, time and duty permitting, I did my bit. This new attitude was a malaise. A French MP said to me one day, 'If it's personal leave, then how the person gets where he wants to go is his business, it is not mine. Is it?' He rubbed his thumb and forefinger together.

'It is little money to spend on a taxi, and a hotel. Little money.'

I said, 'Military Police have been helping each other out for 15 years.'

He shrugged, 'It's not right, this ...'

'Okay then, is it right for me to write up your report and submit it to MP Coy? It takes me an hour, sometimes longer and I have written three reports for you to date. Have I ever let you down?'

'My English is okay spoken but not to write ...'

'Most of the other nationalities here aren't as well paid as the French, and maybe the price of a hotel room isn't little money to them.'

What I'd said made no impression. He sucked on his *Camel* cigarette, crossed his legs, lifted his chin, and began to talk of the cheap but high-quality Persian (made in Germany) rugs in a Hezbollah controlled part of the city.

★★★

When I landed in Dublin—I'd changed out of uniform during the changeover in Heathrow—I was met by Bernadette, Colin and Barry. Barry was five by now and as we sat in the café eating lunch, he turned to Colin and said, 'Don't tell Daddy about the car. It's a surprise.'

'What?' I said.

He put his head down.

In the car park, a lilac car. Mother of Jesus. Like something you'd see a pimp riding in. The Barney mobile.

See what happens when you're out of sight? You come home to a lilac car.

It was a great feeling to be home, especially coming up to Christmas. If I hadn't gone abroad I'd probably have been on duty for Christmas. As it was, I had a couple of weeks off and could relax, catch up on things with my family, really enjoy the festive season. I got so comfortable at home that I didn't know if I was going to be able to leave again—that's something about going home on holiday from a mission abroad —you're doubling up on the goodbyes. In the mornings I'd sit on the sofa, sipping coffee, Barry beside me, watching TV, talking, working his way towards eventually inviting me to join him on the floor to play with his toys.

> 21 Dec: *Diary entry*: Christ, how am I going to go back? I have to. I don't want to break a mission, to throw in the towel. I don't want to do that now, not when I didn't do it before, when I had more reason to.

The day before I was to return to Lebanon I'd gone to see an ear specialist who was acting for the Department of Defence. Some months before this I'd been to see Mr George Fennell, another ear specialist, who used to work for the Department of Defence and for the British Ministry of Defence. He was satisfied, after examining my ears, that I was suffering from tinnitus, and explained the graph lines on my audiograms. He also told me a little about my condition.

I don't know how it's actually possible to determine if a person has tinnitus, if the means to verify its existence are beyond questionable doubt, but I assume that there are tell-tale signs. He was most definite.

The specialist acting on behalf of the Department of Defence had a room that resembled, to my untrained eye, a chamber of horrors; archaic equipment. I was fitted with a headpiece, had tuning forks ringing in each ear, and some other tests. These tests didn't bother me in the least, for I wasn't bluffing, feigning or making my condition out to be worse than it was, and knowing this, and adhering to the truth gave me an inner strength. I'm no angel but listen, I've a face that reads like an open book with large print. You'd see a lie in me from a mile.

On my way home and totally on spec, driving the lilac car, I called into my solicitor to find out if a date for my case to heard in the High Court had been determined. I expected to be waiting a year, perhaps two. Imagine my surprise when the receptionist said, 'Oh yes, 27 January...'

'What? In three weeks?'

'Yes.'

'When were you going to tell me?'

'There's a letter on its way to you. We need the names of two witnesses apart from your wife ...'

'I'm in Lebanon.'

She looked at me, cocking an eyebrow.

'I mean I'm flying back tomorrow ...'

'Oh.'

'Yeah, oh.'

'Will I cancel it?'

I shook my head, 'No, don't do that.'

I went home and rang a friend. He thought for a few moments, said he had the leave roster at his fingertips, and continued, 'You've more leave to take—seven days—run it to nine. They won't count the weekend …' In other words come on back, don't lose the trip.

The next morning I flew to Beirut. The MPs, not a Frenchman, drove me to a meeting point outside Sidon where MP Tyre brought me to Naqoura. The following morning I booked a flight home through *Alpha Tours* in Nahariya. I could have used *Saad Tours* in Beirut again, but Charlie Swing-gate was closing too often on shell alerts for me to feel secure about making the flight. Better to cross the border after work, stay in Mickey's hotel and head for the airport. Julie, through whom I'd booked my ticket, had also included a taxi, that cost, 'little money.'

It was with anxiety and concern that I read the news from home. The Minister of Defence was under pressure, the media lamented the 'greedy soldiers,' making it appear as though we were traitors. More and more cases were being heard in the court and not settled on the steps. Most were won by the claimants, a few lost. The cost of bringing the case into court was a lot more expensive than settling the issue on the steps. TV and radio debates raged—front page headlines.

Crossing the border I went into Mickey's—*Hotel Erna*—he knew me of old. Mickey lived across from the old MP detachment and used to bring over fresh loaves every morning, and in return we'd give him foodstuffs of our own: tins of tuna, chilli con carne, bully beef … stuff you'd want a shredder in your belly to help digest. Frozen meat, too. Except pork, naturally.

The airport taxi arrived at 3am and drove around the suburbs of Nahariya and Akko until the driver had picked his full complement of passengers.

A two-day old edition of *The Jerusalem Post* told of flight delays at Ben Gurion, caused by gulls feeding on the nearby municipal dump and getting sucked into the engines of airplanes. Charlie Swing-gate and bloody birds.

I arrived in the airport in plenty of time, had a coffee and watched a security guard tip around the tiled floor, surreptitiously checking the rubbish bins for bombs and suchlike. I'd no passport and when I presented my blue UN I.D. card, phone calls were made back and forth. UNIFIL had an arrangement in place with Israel whereby its I.D. card was sort of a *laissez-passer*. But Murphy's Law and all that … I was concerned.

I was allowed to proceed after I'd answered every question on the questionnaire. Inane, stupid questions … but that was my season for hearing them … there were many more to come.

CHAPTER 22

Home. To a different type of war zone. The situation regarding the hearing issue was deteriorating further, the eventual cost to the exchequer quoted to run into astronomical figures. I think it was the first time that the Irish nation as a people really stopped to consider the fact that, 'Hey, hang on, *we* have an army? And it *costs!*' Times when the public paused to think of their army: when they were strike busters, binmen, firefighters, bus drivers; or perhaps when tragedy struck in a UN mission or someone was blown to bits in the Glen of Imaal. Soldiers, the common soldier (as I once heard a woman describe the other ranks), were the doormats of Irish society, the ones you wiped your feet on when you wanted your shoes to be clean. But now the common soldier was exercising his common right and the not so common people didn't like it, one bit.

On our way to the High Court, in the Barney mobile, it came over the radio about the probable likelihood of the cases being postponed, that the Minister of Defence was seeking an adjournment of the sittings until October at least of that year. It didn't augur well for my case to be heard. And to make matters worse, while crossing the bridge at Heuston Station the back wing of the Barney mobile sustained damage when the mid-tyre of an articulated lorry brushed against it. No injuries. A mushroom lorry. Ironic, when you think that's what soldiers often complained of—being kept in the dark and fed shite; like mushrooms.

On the day of the case, a Military Policeman from the Curragh accompanied us to Dublin. Witnesses were on call if needed, primarily, I presumed, to vouch for the claimant's presence on the firing ranges. Till now, the majority of cases were being settled outside the court room, but now there was a new and determined approach to bring the cases into court and as such some soldiers were thrown by this new development. They did not want to face into being questioned on the stand, nor have their names appear in the newspapers. Understandably so. This reticence had little to do with whether or not their cases were genuine. Most would never have been in a court room before, or felt the heat of an irate public in their face; or propaganda prepared by the Government and stirred by the Irish media. Hitherto, soldier's wives hadn't always been required to take the stand, but the majority now found themselves in this position, thrust into the heat of battle. This proved too much of an ordeal for a few.

It was a showcase to batter the ordinary soldier, to prick his conscience, to vilify him. If this had happened to any other citizen in the country, questions of the Government might well have been asked by the Human Rights Commission. Members of the public insulted me when I was in uniform. I was shunned by people who knew me. I was invited to leave a pub … but if the Government thought they had men with balls of cotton wool in the army, well, they didn't know their men very well. Errors of judgement in the mists of time had led to this fiasco. Yet, during the days ahead I gained some understanding of the reason behind this ire …

The High Court is an awful place. The innocent are the sun on the surface of the water, the floor is the morass of society: killers, rapists, general scum, in-between are the little fish trying to surface. There are no sharks in this river, only piranha. On its granite walls are bullet marks, the signs of battle from another age. What would old soldiers think of the debacle? Would they think the modern soldier a festering sore on society, be ashamed of him? Would they say, 'At last the tide has turned.'

In the round hall, men in wigs and gowns flurried about like penguins disturbed on a beach. Uniformed soldiers stood around the hallowed walls, in clusters of wives and other witnesses. I studied the court lists that were encased behind glass north and south of the hall. My case was 8th on the list.

Denis Boland, my solicitor, found us and with him was our barrister, Alan Mahon. We spoke for a short while in a room away from the hubbub, and Alan went through my case in detail. Making us aware of the storm that had suddenly and unexpectedly broken and that nothing could now be taken for granted. Denis advised us to sit in on cases in progress to familiarise ourselves with the questions being asked, to take the strangeness out of being in court.

I sat in on one or two cases. One man had left the army and then went to work in a noisy environment for nine years. I listened to this in disbelief. How could he attribute his hearing loss to the army after working in noisy conditions for nine years? The judge wondered too and adjourned proceedings to allow the claimant consult with his solicitor—a hint as subtle as a kick in the arse.

The opposing barrister was a knight of his realm. Intelligent, clever and quietly incisive. He asked a senior NCO if he had other health problems which might adversely affect his army career, and the answer he gave was, 'No.' A few minutes later after some less than probing questions, the barrister said, 'I put it to you that there were other health issues that might affect your career …'

He listed a couple. Within seconds there was an exchange of papers between the sides and the case was settled.

I saw a soldier and his wife who stood in a corner in the rotunda all day, every day, and never stepped inside a court room until it was their turn. He was less than confident in the stand and she worse. It was too big an occasion for them and their lack of confidence, their mildness, their unconvincing testimony—not dishonest, just unconvincing—made it easy for the presiding judge not to rule in their favour.

The days slipped by with my case edging forward. My leave was due to end 9 February. I was to be back at work in Lebanon on that day, a Monday. It looked like I was returning to Lebanon empty-handed and out of pocket, expenses had eaten into my overseas allowance, with the weight of a future court date in my mind. D-Day was Thursday. News broke that all hearing cases after the day's session were to be adjourned until the end of the year. It looked bleak. There was a soldier ahead of me and the day's clock was running down. Endless coffees in the basement café, trying to sit on our nerves.

Later in the hall, Denis Boland approached us again. Denis was a dapper man, and had very likeable qualities. Beside him was our bewigged and gowned barrister Alan. They'd walked away from a couple who were now engaged in a deep discussion, their heads bent towards each other. This was the soldier due in court before us.

Denis and Alan were good at their jobs. They explained to me that we were in for a fight, because the Government was now prepared to contest every case, and they felt that I should know this.

They said they'd leave Bernadette and I alone to talk about it for a few minutes. I tried to remain steady. Our case was next.

'Well, what do you think, Bernadette?' I said.

'It's your call.'

'I didn't say it wasn't, but what do you think?'.

'We've come this far …'

'The witness stand …'

'That doesn't bother me,' she said. It did, of course.

'Keep to the truth. Say yes and no and you'll be grand.'

Money. If I lost … Losing this would leave me skint—no savings and a huge debt. I could walk away, but with tinnitus. And I didn't plant it there. The walk to the car park was too awful to contemplate. I'd a fleeting image of Napoleon's retreat from Moscow.

I looked at Bernadette and thought: I'm wrong to put her through this. Wrong to have her name appear in national newspapers, because win, lose or draw, the country's going to read of the case tomorrow. This and the risk of major financial loss threatened to weaken my resolve.

We walked towards Court 2, climbed the steps.

'We're on,' Denis said. '

The courtroom began to fill. A couple of reporters, an army

captain there to report back to the military hierarchy, some soldiers, experts, civilians. Full-house. We're called to stand when the judge enters. A thin man with sallow features and heavy eyebrows. The opposing barrister is the one whom I'd seen dismantle arguments. He asked the judge Justice Johnson to dismiss the case because the claimant wasn't suing for loss of hearing.

A pre-emptive strike. The Justice said, 'He alleges he has a slight hearing problem which he isn't claiming for, but that he is suffering from noise induced tinnitus. The case will proceed.'

Bernadette was sworn in. Under our barrister's prompts, she said that she'd first noticed a character change in me going back a couple of years. I'd become impatient, irritable, and tired. I'd a disturbed sleep pattern.

'Does he have a problem with noise?'

'He can't stand loud noise; the television, the washing machine …'

'And your social life. How does tinnitus affect this aspect of your life?'

'He avoids places where there is too much noise. It seems a natural thing for him to do.'

'Did he complain to you of a ringing noise in his ears?'

'He mentioned it a few times, but never went overboard about it.'

'No more questions, your honour. '

When the opposing barrister rose to his feet, he coughed and pushed his robe behind him. He didn't ask too many questions, more or less the same as our own barrister.

I gripped Bernadette's hand when she returned to her seat

and said well done. She warned me to speak up. If she heard me mumble she'd do gaol for me. But I'd no intention of going down whimpering. In a quiet moment away from everyone I'd prayed, not to be successful, but to come across as best I could. I walked briskly toward the stand, paused to accord the Judge respect, as required by military regulations, and then assumed my place. I then took the oath. My barrister began questioning, bringing me through my army career, the courses I had been on, my tours of duty abroad. We talked about the source of my complaint.

'Is this noise present as we speak?'

'Yes. But external noise smothers it.'

'How does tinnitus disrupt your life?'

'It affects my sleep pattern. I'm conscious of it during moments that should be silent. I get a little depressed at times, not too down, but more browned off than usual.'

'Talk to us about being on the rifle ranges. What hearing protection do you wear?'

'None. But I believe that protection is coming on stream.'

'Were you ever advised on the danger of exposing your hearing to noise?'

'No.'

He nodded and said, 'Thank you, Mister Malone.'

The state's barrister rose slowly and nodded at the judge. The stenographer situated in front of me nodded. All the best.

'Mister Malone, do you know that a great many people suffer from tinnitus in this country? It is not so uncommon an affliction?'

'I'm not aware of the statistics.'

'Well, there are a lot of people who suffer from tinnitus. And they aren't in court, nor will they be in court.'

I remained silent.

'Well, Mr Malone?'

'What is your question?'

'Do you agree with me that tinnitus is a common affliction?'

'Would these people all have been weapon instructors?'

A ripple of laughter travelled the courtroom, faded quickly, like a door shut against a draught.

'I'll ask the questions, Corporal Malone. So, Mister Malone, how do you cope with your tinnitus?'

'I go to bed exhausted and I usually fall asleep eventually. I lose about two nights sleep every ten days. Usually, usually I get about four to five hours sleep a night, and the noise is the first thing I hear when I waken.'

'Your imagination, perhaps?'

'I call it noise.'

'I suppose like many of your colleagues you listen to a Walkman to drown this ringing?'

'Occasionally. Not often.'

'Have you ever been to a rock concert, a disco for instance?'

'I've been to discos. No rock concerts.'

'Mister Malone, now, tell me, were you ever given cotton wool to put in your ears before going on range practice?'

'Not that can I remember, no.'

'I put it to you that you were.'

'I can't remember.'

'So, it's possible that you were given cotton wool to put in your ears before firing?'

'If I can't remember I can't deny that I wasn't.'

I thought of the sniper Ambrose Bierce wrote of in his short story about a man who dreams of escape as he waits to be hanged on a bridge above a river—grey eyes are keenest. The dreamer as he swam to safety feared the sniper.

'You write, Mister Malone?'

'I do.'

'Well, given that fact then, isn't it to your advantage that you stay awake, that your tinnitus gives you a routine?'

'John B. Keane said: routine is the enemy of creativity.'

As though a switch had been flipped in my head I said to myself: I've had enough of this shit.

'Listen, I shouldn't be here.'

He puckered his lips, and said, 'You mean you'd waive your right to sue for compensation?'

'That's not what I said. I expect to receive compensation. I resent being here, resent the military authorities putting my wife and I through this when there was no need. I attended three army doctors, all of whom told me that there was nothing they could do to treat tinnitus.'

'This is true.'

'They didn't even examine my ears. They didn't want to know. And yet I heard you in court talk about the Irish Tinnitus Association and a masking device that deadens the noise. I wouldn't be here if the doctors had fully investigated my problem, they would have come to realise that my complaint was genuine. You appear to know more about tinnitus than the army's doctors.'

'I would suggest to you that you are only aware of the noise when you listen carefully.'

'No. It is intrusive.'

He pondered my response for a few seconds and then said, 'No further questions, your honour.'

I didn't take the cross-examination personally. He was a good barrister, doing his job.

George Fennell, the audiologist, came across well under the barrister's cross-examination. He mentioned *Hyperacusis*, a decreased ability in a person to tolerate noise. He was cut short when he began to talk of his vast RAF experiences in relation to tinnitus.

No more witnesses called. The silence of the Antarctica when the wind is still and the snow sleeps.

The Judge deliberated. I held my breath and squeezed hard the rim of my seat. Initially, its varnish was cold to my touch, but then the wood warmed. I thought of drinking coffee and smoking a cigar. My nerves ached for a cigar. I thought of lying on a white sandy beach watching the surf come in. *Hurry, hurry, for fuck's sake before the palpitations kill me, before my heart jumps out onto the floor and races a yard before detonating.*

I'd love to be able to take out my noise and show it to people. Irrefutable evidence, 'Listen – this is what it's like.' At last. The silent hush descends to a lower level of hush.

'Mister Malone is a very intelligent man. He presented his evidence well and did not exaggerate his condition. I think the army authorities could have been more sensitive in their dealings with him. He has given excellent service to his country at home and abroad. I find in his favour for £15,000, with costs.'

An outbreak of activity in front of his bench, like crows after the one morsel. Denis shook his clenched fist, and said, 'Yes!'

Bernadette clasped her hands to her face. The handshakes, the 'well done's' passed me by in a blur. I went over and shook George Fennell's hand, because I felt he was the only one who knew for a fact that I had the condition, and fully understood its associated problems. Denis said he needed to talk with me and I followed him to a room and signed a ream of papers. He said he wished more of his witnesses had the same steel.

A day like this mightn't have happened for me yesterday or tomorrow. Today, things had fallen into place. You'd think it had been fated.

'If you need to draw down some money in a hurry, call into my office and ask one of the girls to type up a letter for the bank. The award takes about six weeks to come through.'

He added that he had to run. Which we had to do too as we crossed the road to the car park across the Liffey, to catcalls from passers-by …

'Deaf fuckers,' said one.

We looked behind.

'I thought you were fuckin' deaf …'

Yeah … That's the way it was.

Deaf fuckers.

CHAPTER 23

1 Mar: *Diary entry*: My initial reaction to winning the case is a feeling of justice dispensed. The money is important though inadequate compensation when set against the future costs of counselling, the inability to concentrate for long periods, the lethargy, the aggravation and frustration, mood swings, the depression, sleep deprivation, but it is more important that I won. Vindication.

Compensation—in England you receive £2,000 to £3,000 sterling for mild tinnitus. For disruptive tinnitus you're looking at £10,000 to £15,000 for general damages, and substantially more when other factors are taken into consideration.

Tinnitus is with me as I write. Constant, enduring. For sufferers of this condition there is never a charitable silence.

Attitudes towards tinnitus haven't changed in eight years. People say it's only a bit of noise, get over it. Others don't believe you. Think it's your imagination. Listen. If you don't manage it, you go under …

There is no cure. Ginkgo Biloba, the herb, is supposed to alleviate the condition, and a clinic in one of the Baltic States is said to have a cure. George Fennell was wrong when he said that the ringing noise remained at a constant pitched level. Yes, it is constant, but the pitch fluctuates. When I'm stressed or have a head cold the noise worsens.

***

Money wasn't a deciding factor in my decision to return overseas.

I had an idea that this was my last time to the well. Though I had convinced myself of this before, this time it was different. All that was happening in and outside of the army—the lack of promotion, the court case, being away from my family, poor morale, proved disheartening. I made up my mind around then to leave the army once I'd clocked up 21 years service and qualified for a pension.

A day or so after the case I said my goodbyes to Bernadette and the boys and flew to Heathrow, waited hours then to catch a connecting flight to Ben Gurion airport.

The army had arranged for Netanya Military Police to collect me at the airport and to provide a bed for me at the detachment. The detachment had been relocated to a modern apartment, far removed from the centre of town. In time the detachment would be moved to Jerusalem and Netanya closed down. I was on a slow climb from the high of the court, the ball of anxiety in the pit of my stomach only beginning to unravel. I had the feeling that I'd buried my army career or had gone some way towards it—there were other soldiers who'd received much more compensation than I had and because their cases were settled outside court they hadn't to endure the media or public glare, and it was sometimes forgotten that they'd claimed. Other soldiers went to solicitors as I had done and were found not to have a hearing deficiency or to be suffering from tinnitus. In some cases soldiers went to the solicitor first and not their doctor, which, you know, to me, made absolutely no sense. If you suffer from a condition you try to get it fixed. Compensation is a matter that might or might not follow.

Early next morning I caught a train from Netanya to Nahariya. My travelling companions were mainly young soldiers, men and women, tired and quiet and sullen, heading to the northern territories to serve their country. Olive green uniforms faded and baggy, rough material. I doubt if the Israeli Army uniform on general service has altered much since the early 1950s. The countryside we passed through—I'd thought Israel so clean—outside the Arab areas, saw me taken aback by the dirt and litter along that route. I could have been travelling to Heuston Station, clickety-clacking behind the back gardens of Dublin housing estates. Blue and white carriages, the dust of many days on them, snaked through the landscape, idling through towns...

I stayed that night in Mickey's. I read, slept, walked the beach road and ate in a bar where the service was lousy and the food bland. I felt left out of myself.

In MP Coy I roomed with a chap called Mick. The prefab was old and hard to keep clean. Formica covering the walls, warped and broken, had peeled away in places. Strategically fitted sheets of chipboard kept the rain at bay, almost. The wardrobes and bedside lockers a cold grey steel. Old graffiti in permanent marker. Tops of wardrobe doors bent back from guys forgetting they'd left their keys on the upper shelf, the lock secured. Like old school teachers used to bend ears. A glow in the dark crucifix left behind by my predecessor, water stains on the walls. A plastic kettle I'd bought in Ali's boiled water in ten seconds flat and proved a life-saver on cold damp mornings. The stink of the paraffin heater as the soot on the wire globe burned off, and Mick thinking he'd woken me when he came in late at night. I'd be awake anyway; heading to the loo, or to the empty mess to sit for an hour reading. Sometimes the loneliness was biting.

Electrical storms at sea, lightning forks and jagged spears, eerily illuminating the Moorish keep, the foam of madly stirred waters. Claps of thunder, the driving rain, days when a yellow dust storm blew and the grit tore at your eyes and the dust invaded everywhere. Pervasive.

Beer in Pablo's, draught *Amstel*, his bar restaurant in Mingi Street situated above his antique shop, his sawn-off shotgun under his counter … I was aware that I was the talk of the place among the Irish soldiers who drank there, and I didn't like it. Newspapers had arrived and my name appeared in most of them—facts stated. Stories filtered to Lebanon from home, from people who had been in court.

Isolated. I think that's how I felt. Those first few days after the court case.

John Jeffers stayed in the last room standing on Patrick Street, new accommodation going up all around him, brick-built. John had a very pragmatic way of looking at things and came out now and then with good advice that helped steer my thoughts to quieter waters.

I immersed myself in my work, finishing off a caseload of files, polishing the reports of my colleagues in Traffic. Then a couple of incidents ...

I was in bed one night, lights out, it must have been about 11pm when Hekka, Traffic Section head, arrived into my room. He called me and I flipped my bedside lamp, immediately thinking, 'Major T.A. —shooting?'

'Come, Murt, we have to go.'

'Where?'

'The late crossing. The Duty NCO received a report about drivers who are drinking in Nahariya rec house and they are crossing the border ...'

I smelt a rat.

'Hekka, who reported it?'

A Norwegian MP to a Norwegian shift commander ...

I dressed and joined Hekka, sitting beside him in the cruiser. He drove along the camp road, heading south, and parked at the French lines near the French manned gates and control tower. It was cold and damp. And my thoughts were drifting into high gear.

'Hekka, I don't like this at all.'

'We have the report ...'

I looked down the road and saw the sentry pulling on the metal gates, allowing two cars through, the slap of his hand against the butt of his rifle in salute ... I walked ahead of Hekka and flashed my *Streamlite* at the first car to slow down, saw who was in it and waved them forward to Hekka. *No fuckin' way*, I thought: The drivers were officers. I went to the MP jeep and looked in the back at the Judas Norwegian and other passengers, said hello and asked the Italian MP to breathe into the breathalyser. Talk about shock.

'Are you serious?' the driver said.

'I am.'

I didn't care what the result was, I was making a point. They had it planned that I would stop the two officers in the first vehicle while they'd sit back and enjoy a right snigger. There was bad blood, I knew, between the Norwegians over the MP Coy appointments, and while I didn't know what'd happened in the six months preceding my arrival, I saw this as a conspiracy.

One of the soldiers from the first car came to me and I briefed him. He shook his head and I could tell he was hurting and bemused. He hadn't much drink taken and neither had the officer who'd been driving. There had been trouble between him and some Scandinavian MPs while I was gone, and he felt they were out to make his time a misery.

The officer in question, who'd been breathalysed, complied with my request, signed his copy of the print report of his test. He behaved like a thorough gentleman and I was very proud of the fact that he did. A man of lesser substance might have railed and tried to use his rank to inveigle his way out of trouble, given the onlookers something to talk about. But there was none of this. He carried himself and his rank with great dignity. His bearing was really impressive.

I hadn't much time to dwell upon this incident or its likely consequences, as right outside the MP Coy the patrol had stopped another driver in a cruiser. Under the watchful and discerning eye of the Norwegians I breathalysed him, too. Yeah, he'd been drinking, but again not a lot. It must be said of the Scandinavians that drink driving is anathema to them, not drinking per se— these were for the most part civilian policemen who quite often in their home duty encountered road carnage attributable to drink and drugs. Perhaps they could not understand the ambivalence of the Irish in the face of proven statistics.

Another night, Hekka called me, acting yet again on a tip-off. He told me its nature and I said, 'I don't think this is our baby. We're here on call-out for emergency purposes, not to deal with routine stuff, Hekka.'

But he was the officer and he was rushing me out the door, no debate. We drove to the French lines where a Land Cruiser had just parked. The driver got out. He'd been drinking. He wore civvies.

I went to him and said, 'May I see your I.D. please?'

His cheeks reddened, lips tightening till they were sharp pink blades, the chin diving in a little.

'I have no I.D.' he said, patting his shirt pockets.

Hekka said, holding the breathalyser to the man's face, 'Breathe.'

Breathtaking diplomacy.

The officer in broken English said he was French, a CO. He went on about diplomatic immunity. Now, I understood what he meant —officers like him thought they had and they usually did have, a sort of untouchable status. Unfortunately I didn't recognise him, nor did Hekka, not that rank carried any privileges in his eyes when it came to driving with alcohol in your blood system. He wanted the officer's breath.

'Breathe,' Hekka repeated.

The officer shook his head, really getting pissed.

'Hekka, let's check his I.D. and put in a report ...'

If he was who he claimed to be, he'd receive the report himself, and write back to the sender—all have a good giggle about it in the mess.

'I will report you,' the officer said, pointing his forefinger.

'Breathe, you must breathe …'

Fuck.

In the end, searching for compromise, we accompanied him to his quarters a short walk away. He opened the door, found his I.D. card and showed it to us, saying, 'Now, get out…'

Hekka said, 'Do I need to write what he said?'

That was it. The officer made a call and the French guard arrived with a junior officer, surrounding us. They pushed against us with their rifles, acting under a drunken officer's command. In effect, we were under arrest, for doing our job, which was stopping people from breaking the law. The junior officer was trying to calm things. The French officer made a move towards me with his hands raised and I brushed them apart, creating the perfect opening for an uppercut. I wouldn't have done it better if planned. He was completely startled and stood back to look at me. He'd a head of steam and by now I had one, too. He wanted back in his bedroom cum office and he wasn't going there, no way. One of my colleagues arrived and he and the French officer talked at length. My colleague did the most sensible thing, that should have been done at the start—retreat and put in a report. In hindsight, at the outset, we should have slapped the officer in the slammer in MP Coy.

After that incident I switched off and relaxed for the rest of the trip. I'd had enough. I typed up my reports and went on speed checks, taking myself out of the office more so than before. Appearing to be proactive. Hekka was sore about what happened and when he saw the French officer making his way across the small square in MP Coy he walked in front of him, not saluting, a 100 per cent pure insult to an officer. Daring him to open his mouth and complain. I would have saluted him. Why? Out of respect for his rank. I never saluted an officer as a person—it was never a personal thing—I respected the rank he carried, what he had earned, and it was that which was worthy of respect. Hekka was civilian police operating in and under a military code. This zero tolerance business was a pointless exercise, trying to wash the grey areas white or darken them black. There'll always be grey areas. It should be called the bullshit zone, where nothing is clear cut.

That conflict between Military Police and the French was one of several incidents that occurred between them during that tour of duty. Other fractious incidents occurred at the two main gates situated north and south of Naqoura camp, when the French guard unnecessarily hassled Military Police as they drove in and out. Our Polish MPs had shot and lightly wounded an Irish soldier in the hospital grounds while on pest control, killing cats …

And then the smuggling was still in progress. This time the smuggling route was toward Beirut. Traders along Mingi Street reported each other for smuggling beer and spirits in UNIFIL trucks. Lightning searches of these trucks found them to be empty or carrying only UNIFIL property. Jesse, a man who supplied the messes with beer, spirits, wine, cigarettes, cigars, and who had served in the South Lebanese Army, along with a couple of other traders, kept me up to speed on what was going on in UNIFIL. This relationship with traders had built up over my previous four trips to Lebanon. He told me about Lebanese customs who had stopped two Irish soldiers smuggling contraband in Sidon, on their way to Beirut. He never put me astray with information, though nothing he ever told me would have fastened to anyone in a court of law.

'They weren't reported,' Jesse said, exhaling cigarette smoke. He had unruly black hair, was about 30, and a smile that occasionally slipped into a slight sneer whenever he snorted in disbelief at how little I knew.

'The customs kept it for themselves, hush, hush, see?'

Later, I heard, not from Jesse, that Lebanese customs officers were under investigation for corruption. Jesse himself, when the Polish customs finally got the finger out and clamped down hard on the Polish rotation, bought back at sale price the alcohol his Polish customers had purchased from him—troops due home on the 2nd and 3rd chalks? Other traders wouldn't buy back their stock. 'Tough,' they said. In Arabic.

During a speed check outside Tyre with Timu, he took out his silver Cannon camera and photographed scenery, while I removed the speed gun from its case and clipped documentation to a blue hand board.

A couple of UNIFIL trucks lumbered past, within the speed limit. There was a lone man working on a building site giving us hard looks and I said, 'Timu, put away the camera.'

In Tyre itself, I parked outside Yousef's the tailor's, where Timu had gone to check if a suit or whatever was ready for collection, when this UN interpreter for the Tyre region rapped on my window. I hadn't seen him since 1986. He didn't know me then, so he didn't recognise me now.

'… I have a report of a UNIFIL jeep—the soldiers were taking photographs of a Hezbollah camp.'

As he was speaking he was looking in the back of the jeep. Timu's camera was in the glove compartment. He saw the speed gun's grey aluminium case …

'Is that your camera?'

'That's a radar gun … speed camera.'

'Aha.'

'Have you a registration number?'

He said it and though he gave a wrong digit, I knew it was us.

'Well,' I said, 'if I see that vehicle around, I'll pull it over. Okay?'

When Timu returned I told him what had happened. He and I knew that this was a sensitive issue, one that arseholes with nothing better to do would exact a lot of mileage from.

He was worried, but to be honest I was more pissed off than worried. I was tired of having to make sure nobody had anything on me, to put the final nail in the coffin of my career.

'Listen, take the film out of your camera and throw it away. Put in a new one and take a few pictures when and where I tell you, right?'

'Right.'

I was thinking that when he arrived in Naqoura someone would confiscate his camera and have the film developed. He was starting out on his travels abroad and this sort of thing. Well, zero tolerance with Finns and all that …

'Now, when you're brought in for questioning say that you were using the speed gun and not the camera. Your camera's silver, the radar gun is the same colour.'

He nodded.

'Now, I'll be asked if you used the camera, and I'm going to say that I didn't see you. If you're told different, it's a lie. You're a cop. Come on, you know what to do.'

An Irish soldier was tasked with the job of investigating the circumstances He was with the SIS.

'Murt,' he said, going on to say that the area photographed was a Hezbollah tower block.

'Jesus, I don't know. Why would anyone photograph a tower block?'

He smiled, 'They want to see him tomorrow and the speed gun.'

'Who wants to see him?' '

'The Hezbollah. We're driving to the tower block.'

'Well, we used the speed gun.'

'Did he use a camera?'

'Unless he took it out behind my back ...'

'It's a yes or a no question.'

'No.'

'Fine,' he smiled.

The Hezbollah heads weren't convinced when they saw the speed camera, but they let the issue slide. Well, what else could they do? Timu was saved from receiving a reprimand. A telling reminder of how dangerous it is to photograph even innocuous looking scenery in a war zone. Lebanon could fool you into thinking it wasn't a theatre of war: sun, lengthy periods of calm, the routine of daily life and then, boom ...

★★★

The Minister for Defence, Michael Smith, visited Naqoura, and Phil detailed the Irish MPs to be in the Blue Beret, in Camp Tara, to meet him and the Chief of Staff, Gerry MacMahon.

It was a morale boosting trip.

The thin attendance drove home how the swingeing cutbacks had left a mere skeletal crew of personnel in Naqoura. Gerry talked to myself and my colleagues, spoke of the threat to the army by the ongoing hearing crisis, that the force might be sizeably reduced as a consequence.

'I mean I have tinnitus and it doesn't cause me a problem,' he said.

'Well, I have it too and it is a problem. Ask my roommate ...'

It was speech time.

My colleague John looked at me, covered his eyes and shook his head, smiling. The Minister offered his hand and I shook it. Why not? If I'd lost my case I still would have taken his hand.

A week or so later I read in the newspapers about IR£10,000 increase in annual salary for the brass and higher echelon civil service staff. Not really too concerned about the army having to downsize after all.

***

Saint Patrick's Day. I was on traffic control duty in the new Camp Shamrock, behind the now demolished Gallows Green. I think Larry Gogan was out or it could have been Gerry Ryan, or Pat Kenny. Maybe they were all visiting. Miserable weather. Later that evening back at base I was invited into the Finnish sauna and there I lashed myself with fronds and got pissed on Soulmaster vodka and I didn't give a pair of fucks about anything.

A question was popped at me.

'Will you be serving in another mission?'

'Maybe.'

By now though I had had enough of UNIFIL—the cutbacks, its ineffectiveness, absences from home, Leb fatigue I suppose. I'd just had it up to my eyes with everything and I was no longer finding myself a dedicated soldier, but from experience I had at last learned not to say, 'Never again.'

As it turned out, if I had, I'd have gotten it right.

EPILOGUE

In 1998, a day or so after arriving home, Barry and I brought Trudy the dog for a walk across the Curragh plains. It was a fine May morning. Barry was quiet in himself, questionless for too long, and so I said, 'What's up?'

He'd heard but appeared intent on ignoring me. He jumped in a puddle of rainwater, splashed a couple of times, staining his jeans with mud spatters. He was about five. Trudy dived into furze bushes after a rabbit.

'Won't you not go to Lebanon any more?' Barry said. He said this quietly in a quiet moment. A May breeze stirred the grass, the mountains clear and vibrant with heather, the skies a perfect blue. A lone hawthorn stood out stark and virginal white against the yellow furze.

'No, I won't.'

'Promise.'

'Okay, I promise.'

He cheered a little after that and ran into the trail between the furze, calling Trudy, slipping once on the pocked earth, divots kicked from it by horses on their way to the all-weather gallops.

In a month's time he would be struck down with meningitis, necessitating a stay in Our Lady's Hospital for Sick Children, in

Crumlin. The horrid anxiety as we waited to hear the test results, watching Barry lying listlessly, was awful. Not knowing which of the two strains of meningitis he had: viral or bacterial … we were worried out of our minds.

Our sheer relief upon finding out that he was fortunate, the pain of seeing another couple in the corridor whose little daughter wasn't so lucky, and hadn't survived. I was glad to be at home when Barry fell ill. I could have been away, serving in the Leb or elsewhere. The incident strengthened my resolve not to travel abroad again. It was me who held Barry firmly, talked to him as the doctor carried out the lumber puncture in the lower back, me he clung to as the long needle bit deep into him. For that one time I was with him—I had not been there for his birth, his christening, but now I was—there for him. It was about time I faced into my responsibilities as a father, a family man, to put the army in second place, to relegate my personal and professional ambitions. And though I loved the travelling abroad, had an affinity with the Middle East, was delighted with this aspect of the army, the cultures I became acquainted with, the friends I made, it was time to bring that chapter of my life to an end.

I stopped applying for overseas services, and I'd be lying if I said I didn't suffer a pang whenever trips to Bosnia, Cyprus, Lebanon and Eritrea came round, that the feet didn't itch. Whereas Bernadette and Colin had left it up to me to decide on travel overseas, Barry had taken away that choice.

Time moved on. Ireland's involvement with UNIFIL ended in November 2001, leaving behind in Naqoura a tiny administration cell. 47 Irish peace-keepers died during the army's involvement in Lebanon. Controversy wages over the circumstances of a few of these deaths. There is the missing soldier, presumed dead, and his comrade slain in their post. There is McAleavy and his cold blooded murder of three comrades. And others too, where family members still seek the truth. Perhaps it's there. If they feel a pull inside to query, to probe, then they should. The murderer of two Irish soldiers, Smallhorn and Barrett, sells ice-cream for a living in Detroit. The incident was recently the subject of a documentary on RTE television. The murderer, Barzi, supposedly shot the Irish soldiers to avenge the death of his brother during a gun battle with Irish soldiers some days previously.

***

I only watched the UNIFIL Commemoration Parade pass along O'Connell Bridge on 25 November 2001 for a few minutes, because I dislike military parades, because you know, such pomp and ceremony is a gilded sham and no less. Propaganda exercises—look at how wonderful we are and all the good that we did? Jesus … give me a break. Prayers and hymns in the Garden of Remembrance are different. That is where you pay real respect, where you honour and lend true and honest memory to those who paid the highest sacrifice. Not a rifle should sound there nor a sword be unsheathed nor a command issued. *The Last Post* by a lone bugler says it all. It is a time for reflection, a time for prayer.

My experiences in Lebanon prompted me to write two novels set in the country. *After Kafra* and *The Broken Cedar*. Short stories like *Old Ground* broadcast by RTE Radio 1, and the soon to be published *Truths*, are fictional tales but realistic. I expect this book to be my last literary excursion to Lebanon. It is time to move on.

Reactions to my writings about Lebanon have been mixed and varied. If one in ten soldiers had bought either book each would have been a best-seller. If one in ten people in my home town bought a book it would also have made the bestseller lists. The fact that they didn't revealed apathy not alone in the army but also in the general public concerning Ireland's role in Lebanon. This isn't a whinge, it's a simple fact. Both novels were critically acclaimed pieces of work, and heralded in Australia, Britain and the States. And I'm very proud of them, because I know where they come from and so too does the discerning reader.

My thoughts of UNIFIL these days are probably best explained by the following ...

The basic concept of the UN is fine, needed, and idealistic, but as an organisation I think it needs to be completely dismantled and restructured:

While surfing the net I chanced upon an article which interested though did not surprise me. An Indian member of UNIFIL had given an interview to an Israeli newspaper in which he said that four Indian members of UNIFIL helped Hezbollah carry out the abduction of three IDF soldiers in October 2000.

Although this type of action would be condemned by UNIFIL commanders, there seems to be some anecdotal evidence to suggest that a small number of peacekeepers have been unable to maintain their neutrality, as this Indian case showed.

UNIFIL'S impartiality, according to this article, had been called into question since this specific allegation surfaced concerning the possible bribery of UNIFIL personnel facilitating the kidnapping, and the refusal of UN personnel to cooperate in the Israeli investigation of the kidnapping.

This startled me, as it was also a kidnapping that sparked off the conflict this summer. We have now seen history repeat itself—soldiers abducted—and this time the Israelis went to war. As I write, news is breaking of the deaths of four UN observers killed when an Israeli shell hit their bunker. Nothing changes, except the date. The news saddened and sickened me.

***

Numb. Slightly disorientated, that's how I felt upon leaving the army after 21 years service. It'd been a difficult decision and the last two years in the army had been particularly hard for me. I saw the writing on the wall regarding promotion. From near misses to a fall down the selection ladder. I'd always felt that my commitment to overseas did not receive the recognition it deserved when and where it mattered. On two occasions when there were no volunteers I answered the call. In the cold light of day this counted for nothing.

Bitter? I couldn't hand on heart give a hoot. The majority of my MP friends have left the unit, transferred to other units or out of the army. Those few remaining in the unit I still meet, talk to and have good time for. We can pick up the threads of a conversation as if we'd spoken yesterday and not three years ago. I passed on my presentation, requesting that a donation be presented to the Army Benevolent Fund. Sparing myself the cant. Thank you very much.

First day on my re-birth into Civvie World I enjoyed a double espresso in a café. It should have been a double whiskey but drink sometimes brings out my Mr Hyde. I seldom write with alcohol coursing through my veins as it can cause dangerous writing. I consoled myself with the knowledge that I had been damn right to leave the army and searched inwardly for vindication. It was slow in coming. Then I discerned an inner voice from a rush of them above the tinnitus. Haven't you a *wee* pension, two novels published and another on the way? Now, as a civvie, you can grow your hair long, sprout a nose-ring, an earring. You can do with you whatever you want.

Midway into the espresso I went deep in reverie: Long ago, on a bright and sunny August morning, I dilly-dallied on a lawn near McDonagh Barracks in the Curragh Camp, asking myself a question—will I or won't I join up? A hefty scent of gardenia freshened the air. I said a prayer and flicked a coin: best of three, my choice always harps. Harps. At that time I said, sure, I'd give it a week and see how it goes.

I was signed up, sworn in and issued with white underpants that had enough ball room to hold a Christy Moore concert, a bristle shaving brush, a razor, green overalls and grey woollen socks that itched and rode up to meet the underpants.

I thought too, in that miserable little café, passing traffic a river of metal, of the time spent away from my family, my sons. How none of it could ever be replaced, not a second. And to know that I'd volunteered to leave them behind. Was it all worth it? Granted, the money enticed and it helped and travelling overseas prised me away from the maddening tedium and general uselessness of daily army life. But was it all worth it? No.

The time and things I shared with Barry showed what I had

missed out on with Colin. Too much service abroad is detrimental to the family. It is difficult enough to keep the stitches together in a relationship without absences of six months occurring on a frequent basis. My marriage has been fortunate to survive. That it has so far has been down to my wife, Bernadette. Without her I wouldn't have been able to give and honour those commitments to my country when it asked me to serve abroad.

A red line drawn through my details in the unit record book: LA 141 – 847077 Cpl Malone M. A space closed in the ranks. Listening to a new reveille, armed only with severance papers and a civilian suit which the army issues its soldiers when they retire. Called the *Martin Henry* it was either take it or approximately €12 in lieu. What sort of suit does a tailor fashion for a dozen euros?

I can tell you now that it lasted a single wear.

Barry once asked me, 'What's a patriot?' A patriot to me is someone who doesn't dump rubbish along the side of the road, or smash gravestones, or drink himself into A&E or a fatal car accident. A patriot respects himself, his people, his country. It is more than saying, 'Hup the IRA, and 'Come on, Ireland...' Indeed, perhaps he is someone who doesn't sue? Or someone who does not misappropriate taxpayers' money? Or someone who does not jump through legal loopholes in order to avoid paying tax. I gave him a watered down version of the above.

He looked at me and said, 'Were the soldiers who died in Lebanon patriots, Da?'

'They were serving their country. What do you think?'

'Yeah, they were.'

I felt like having another espresso but the café was closing. The girl sweeping the floor around my feet asked if I was feeling okay. I was going to ask who was Okay, but instead said I was grieving. She said sorry for your troubles. I said it wasn't the worse kind of grieving. She thought it wise to afford me distance and angled the brush in easy position from which to bayonet me, if necessary.

What of my UN medals, ribbons and numerals? Barry has them. He keeps them out of sight, along with my blue beret and UN cap badge. When I told him I was writing this book he said, 'Will you write about how you weren't around when I was born?'

'Do you think I should?'

'You might as well.'

'Okay, I will.'

He thought for a moment. His fair hair long, his electric guitar resting across his lap. 13 years old.

'Do you think Lebanon will ever let go of you?'

How do you explain that now and then the past decides to hold you prisoner—the images of death and carnage, the good occasions, the freshness and beautiful experiences of those first trips, friendships, later the disillusionment, the attitudes of others, stifled ambition, inequality and unfairness? All of that? It's not so much that I spent five terms serving abroad, that I was in Lebanon, but more that Lebanon was in me, and it always will be.

And of all the ghosts that haunt, it is the ones within that sometimes scare the most.

INDEX

INDEX

MORE NON-FICTION FROM MAVERICK HOUSE

SIEGE AT JADOTVILLE

THE IRISH ARMY'S FORGOTTEN BATTLE
BY DECLAN POWER

The Irish soldier has never been a stranger to fighting the enemy with the odds stacked against him. The notion of charging into adversity has been a cherished part of Ireland's military history.

In September 1961 another chapter should have been written into the annals, but it is a tale that lay shrouded in dust for years.

The men of A Company, 35th Irish Infantry Battalion, arrived in the Congo as a UN contingent to help keep the peace. For many it would be their first trip outside their native shores. Some of the troops were teenage boys, their army-issue hobnailed boots still unbroken.

A Company found themselves tasked with protecting the European population at Jadotville, a small mining town in the southern Congolese province of Katanga. It fell to them to try and protect people who later turned on them.

On 13 September 1961,the bright morning air was shattered by the sound of automatic gunfire.This was to be no Srebrenica. Though cut off and surrounded, the men of Jadotville held their ground and fought...

To order this book go to www.maverickhouse.com

MORE NON-FICTION FROM MAVERICK HOUSE

THE GENERAL AND I

THE UNTOLD STORY OF MARTIN CAHILL'S HOTDOG WARS

By Wolfgang Eulitz

The General and I is the gripping story of an ordinary man's struggle against a criminal psychopath.

Entrepreneur Wolfgang Eulitz worked hard to set up his hot dog business on Dublin's Leeson Street.

But after four years of successful trading and witnessing the chaos and characters of the city's club scene, Martin Cahill appeared and tried to muscle in on his lucrative business. The hot dog wars had begun.

"At the end of his outstretched hands he held a gun, which he now aimed directly at my head. These thugs were here for more than just money. These thugs belonged to Martin Cahill, alias 'The General'."

In this extraordinary account of his encounters with the notorious General, Eulitz gives an insight into Cahill's ruthless character and reveals him to be a cruel, sadistic and dangerous thug.

To order this book go to www.maverickhouse.com

NIGHTMARE IN LAOS
by Kay Danes

Hours after her husband Kerry was kidnapped by the Communist Laos government, Kay Danes tried to flee to Thailand with her two youngest children, only to be intercepted at the border.

Torn away from them and sent to an undisclosed location, it was then that the nightmare really began. Forced to endure 10 months of outrageous injustice and corruption, she and her husband fought for their freedom from behind the filth and squalor of one of Laos' secret gulags.

Battling against a corrupt regime, she came to realise that there were many worse off people held captive in Laos—people without a voice, or any hope of freedom.

Kay had to draw from the strength and spirit of those around her in order to survive this hidden hell, while the world media and Australian government tried desperately to have her and Kerry freed before it was too late and all hope was lost.

For Kay, the sorrow and pain she saw people suffer at the hands of the regime in Laos, where human rights are non-existent, will stay with her forever, and she vowed to tell the world what she has seen. This is her remarkable story.

MORE NON-FICTION FROM MAVERICK HOUSE

HEROIN
A TRUE STORY OF DRUG ADDICTION, HOPE AND TRIUMPH
BY JULIE O'TOOLE

Heroin is a story of hope; a story of a young woman's emergence from the depths of drug addiction and despair.

Julie O'Toole started using heroin in her mid-teens. A bright young girl, she quickly developed a chronic addiction and her life spiralled out of control. Enslaved to the drug, Julie began shoplifting to feed her habit before offering to work as a drug dealer for notorious gangsters.

Julie was eventually saved by the care and support of a drugs counsellor, and by her own strength to endure.

Heroin is a tale of how a young girl became a victim of her surroundings. Julie's story takes us from Dublin's inner city to London and America, and gives an insight into how anyone can become a victim of circumstances.

With honesty and insight, Julie tells of the horror and degradation that came with life as a drug addict, and reveals the extraordinary strength of will that enabled her to conquer heroin addiction and to help others do the same.

To order this book go to www.maverickhouse.com